A HISTO

LEONARD JOHNSTON

# A
# HISTORY
# OF
# ISRAEL

SHEED AND WARD
LONDON AND NEW YORK

FIRST PUBLISHED 1964
SHEED AND WARD LTD
33 MAIDEN LANE
LONDON W.C.2
AND
SHEED AND WARD INC
64 UNIVERSITY PLACE
NEW YORK 3

NIHIL OBSTAT: HUBERTUS RICHARDS, S.T.L., L.S.S.
CENSOR DEPUTATUS
IMPRIMATUR: ✠GEORGIUS L. CRAVEN,
EPŪS SEBASTOPOLIS VIC. GEN.
WESTMONASTERII, DIE 23ª DEC. 1963.

*The* Nihil obstat *and* Imprimatur *are a declaration that a book or pamphlet is considered to be free from doctrinal or moral error. It is not implied that those who have granted the* Nihil obstat *and* Imprimatur *agree with the contents, opinions or statements expressed.*

*This book is set in 11 on 13 pt. Linotype Baskerville*

*Made and printed in Great Britain by
William Clowes and Sons, Limited, London and Beccles*

# CONTENTS

# 1

## HISTORY AND BIBLE HISTORY

WITHIN the space of a generation, our view of the ancient world has been transformed. In the last fifty years, excavations have brought to light buried cities and the debris of their life—pottery, tools, weapons; silent memorials which skilled interpretation can with increasing sureness still make speak to us. More explicitly, the written records of the past speak to us; the chronicles of kings, the great myths and legends, legal and commercial documents, and even private correspondence. All of this has made it possible for us to know almost as much about life in ancient Egypt, for example, as we do about life in medieval England. We know how people lived; and what is more important, we know how they felt and thought.[1]

---

[1] There is an abundance of literature today in which the results of archaeological research are made available. To mention only a few of the more useful and more accessible:

J. B. Pritchard (ed.), *Ancient Near Eastern Texts*, 1st ed. (1950) (to which reference is made in this book); and

This is particularly true of the world of the ancient Near East—of which world Israel was part. For the history of Israel, however, the Bible itself remains the primary source. But for this very reason, it is all the more important to be clear on the character of this source material, and the way it is to be used in reconstructing the picture of Israel's past.[2]

The first thing we have to bear in mind is that history is never merely a matter of recording a complete list of events in the past. The events have to be sifted, selected and arranged in a meaningful pattern before we have history properly so called. Moreover, the selection and arrangement of the facts will vary with the specific object the historian has in mind, according to the type of history he is writing—economic,

---

2nd ed. (1955). (Abbreviated in subsequent references as *ANET*.)

J. Finegan, *Light from the Ancient Past*, 2nd ed. (1959)

D. W. Thomas (ed.) *Documents from Old Testament Times* (1958)

W. F. Albright, *From the Stone Age to Christianity*, 2nd ed. (1957)

W. F. Albright, *The Archaeology of Palestine*, Pelican (1954)

L. H. Grollenberg, *Atlas of the Bible* (1956).

[2] On all the following, the encyclical *Divino Afflante Spiritu* (CTS translation, *Biblical Studies*, especially §§ 38–44) will be found an invaluable summary of the principles.

social or political history, for example. The type of history we have in the Bible is one which is often called "religious history". It is written out of the conviction that God has revealed himself in Israel's history, and the facts have been selected, arranged and presented in such a way as to make this clear.[3] In a sense, one could even say that it is not history at all, but theology; except that the theology is inseparably linked with the national history. An indication of this attitude can be seen in the terminology used by the earliest, Hebrew, editors of the Bible; they describe the collection of books from Joshua to Kings, not as history, but as "prophecy"—that is to say, they are to be seen as part of the same general category as the great preachers of God's word such as Isaiah or Jeremiah. The primary purpose of history in the Bible is not to convey information about the past for its own sake, but to proclaim God's great deeds.

This alone will make a great difference to the way we approach the Bible as a historical source. But moreover, we have to reckon not only with a specific type of history—and the conventions to be expected from this type—but with the sources which were available to the authors in carrying out their aim. For the historical works **of the Old Testament are not "books" in the**

[3] Cf. G. E. Wright, *God Who Acts* (1952).

modern sense of the term—completely original compositions of individual authors. They are much more like compilations from already existing material. More will be said about this in the course of the history which follows; but some general characteristics may be noted here in order to make it clear in what spirit we are to approach it.

Most of the information given in the Bible— and this is particularly true of the earliest history, that found in the Pentateuch—was handed down in the first place by word of mouth. Oral tradition is popular, picturesque, anecdotal. It was not an official, formal record of events, but was handed down in local or family groups for reasons peculiar to that group. It is picturesque; it is the story of "the remembered past",[4] and it must then be, precisely, memorable; if it were dull and ordinary, it would not have been handed down. It is anecdotal; it will not give a complete and balanced view of whole periods of history, but will conserve the intimate detail, the colourful and striking episode; it will deal with individuals rather than with vast anonymous groups, and it will tell their story, more-

[4] The phrase is from J. L. McKenzie's *The Two-Edged Sword*, which also gives a good account of this subject, pp. 60–71.

over, in the form of isolated events rather than as a connected history.

In the course of oral transmission, variations will develop in the account; not so much because of fallibility of memory—the powers of memory of non-literary people are notorious and indeed exaggerated—as because of variation of interests on the part of the people among whom the stories circulated. Examples of this in the Bible are numerous: there are two accounts of Abraham's covenant with God (Gen. 15 and 17); two accounts of his promised heir (Gen. 17.15–21 and 18.9–15); two different explanations of the name "Israel" (Gen. 32.28 and 35.9–10); Joseph is taken to Egypt by the Midianites (Gen. 37.28) or by Ishmaelites (Gen. 37.25), while Judah (37.26) or Reuben (37.21) tries to save him.

Another characteristic of popular tradition is what may be described as a homely sort of "philosophizing"—simple, unscientific attempts to provide "explanations" for things. We see this in the Bible in the interpretations given to proper names: Abraham, father of a multitude; Jacob, the supplanter, and so on; explanations which have little or no etymological value whatever. A combination of this and the personal feature of oral traditions noted above results in a similar kind of "popular ethnology"—stories aimed at providing an explanation of Israel's relationship with neighbouring peoples: with the Edomites (Gen. 36.40–43); the Ishmaelites (Gen. 25.12–16); the Moabites and Ammonites (Gen. 19.37–8).

A similar device is adopted with many place-names: Bethel (Gen. 28.19); Penuel (Gen. 32.30); Mizpah (Gen. 31.49). But this point gives us further insight into the character of the material we are dealing with. We have already noted the characteristic of popular tradition that it consists originally of isolated anecdotes. This is evident, for example, in the stories of the Patriarchs in Genesis; individual stories may be beautifully told, but as biography or history the account as a whole is not very satisfying; it is scrappy and lacking in coherence. But one factor which does provide something of a guiding thread to the narrative is the regular reference to the places at which the Patriarchs paused in their wanderings—these place-names plot their movements and punctuate the narrative. This gives us a glimpse of the actual manner in which many of these stories were conserved; they were handed on by people of a particular place who treasured the memory of their ancestors' connection with that place.

Moreover, many of these places were "holy places". A place was said to be "holy" because of some supernatural event which took place

there, usually a vision or an appearance of God.[5]
And it was an important part of the tradition of
such sanctuaries to preserve the memory of the
event on which its title to holiness rested.

The whole process is probably best understood
in the light of this passage from Deuteronomy
(26.1–8):

> When you come into the land which the Lord
> your God shall give you, you shall take some
> of the first-fruits of the produce of the earth.
> You shall put it in a basket and go to the place
> chosen by God . . . and you shall say: My
> father was a wandering Aramean who went
> down to Egypt; few in number he took refuge
> there, but he became a great nation, mighty
> and many. The Egyptians ill-treated us, op-
> pressed us and inflicted harsh service on us.
> We called on Yahweh, the God of our fathers,
> and Yahweh heard our voice, he saw our
> misery, our distress and oppression. And he
> brought us out of Egypt with mighty hand
> and outstretched arm . . .

This text is practically a summary of the
events from Abraham to the entry into Canaan;
and, as the context shows, it is an act of faith to
be recited on a great religious occasion. It is
easy to see how, from such a summary confession,

[5] Cf. R. de Vaux, *Ancient Israel*, pp. 276–7, 289.

the narrative material of the Pentateuch would develop—and develop, no doubt, in the same context and the same spirit; that is to say, as a confession of faith made at a holy place on the occasion of some great feast commemorating God's great deeds.

This, then, is the nature of the material which makes up our Bible history: separate stories conserved by groups who were particularly connected with the people concerned or at places which had some particular interest in these traditions; eventually gathered into minor collections; and finally into the major collections of which the present historical corpus of the Old Testament is composed; and at every stage intended primarily as a proclamation of the faith of Israel.

All of this is by now quite generally understood; it has, after all, been common teaching for the past twenty years. But there still seems to be often a reluctance to come to grips with the facts of Israel's history. This appears to be particularly true at a certain stage of biblical education, when the first principles have been grasped: that the Bible is the story of salvation, the story of God's great deeds, that God has come amongst men. These can become so many *clichés* tossed around indefinitely in an atmosphere of vague enthusiasm if they are not linked with a firm appreciation of what actually did happen. It is almost as if we were afraid that too close contact with the reality would break the spell and dispel illusions. But in religion, the proper name for illusion is superstition. To view the past through a veil of romanticism may usually be only harmless fantasy; but to view Israel's history like this is fatal, for the one thing which is above all important about it is that it really happened. To think of God acting in the world of human experience is inspiring; but this truth is obscured and devalued if we minimize the reality of the events in which God's action showed itself.

A history of Israel, then, such as this book aims to be, is rather different from a Bible History. The Bible itself is the principal source for this history; indeed, the reader is presumed to have the Bible text in mind all through the pages which follow; but that text must be interpreted. The information it gives can be tested by the abundant information which is now available concerning the history of the ancient Near East in general. Its style and conventions can be judged not merely by our knowledge of the writers' purpose and source, but also by our present knowledge of other ancient Near-Eastern literature.

This task of interpretation is not always easy, and it will be realized that not all difficulties are yet solved. Certain questions, indeed, are not even asked; whether the sun stood still for Joshua, for example, is matter for the literary critic rather than for the historian. To other questions, the answer can sometimes be only hypothetical. There is no point in minimizing these uncertainties; it is part of an adult understanding of the Bible that we should wish to know just what is certain and what is still doubtful.

Equally, however, there is no point in exaggerating the difficulties. The nation of Israel is a fact of history as real as the people of Rome or Egypt. After all the necessary qualifications have been made in regard to the biblical narrative, it still remains true that it does deal with history —it is not simply a parable or an allegory. And a history of Israel does not destroy the value of the Bible, but on the contrary enables us to see more accurately its precise meaning and value. The Bible has its own special purpose and its own approach, and its own infinite value. We shall appreciate these better by seeing the history of Israel not through a rosy glow of vague religious enthusiasm, but in the light of facts. Just as a clearer appreciation of our Lord's humanity makes his divine nature stand out with even greater force, so the more we can see

Israel as a nation like any other, rooted in the real conditions of place and time, the more the uniqueness of this people and the reality of God's action on them will come to us with inescapable power.

# ISRAEL'S ANCESTORS

---

HISTORY, properly speaking, deals with nations—groups of people with some recognizable corporate identity, with some degree of unity and organization. The nation which we call Israel does not exist in this sense before the thirteenth century BC. But clearly a nation does not spring into existence overnight; and no history would be complete without at least some consideration of the roots from which it sprang.

## 1. THE WORLD OF THE PATRIARCHS

The Israelites traced their origin back to a certain Abraham who lived in "Ur of the Chaldees", at a date which we can put somewhere in the second millennium BC.

It is a surprising fact that as we grow older— as the world grows older—our idea of time seems to contract. There was once a time when dates like 2000 BC or 1300 BC sounded incredibly old, so remote as to be hardly real. But we live in an age which can speak of a thousand light-years and know that it is just the twinkling of a star; we know that the planet on which we live has a history going back several millions of years; and we know that man, appearing on this planet less than a million years ago, is a comparative newcomer.

In this perspective, 2000 BC is practically modern. Man's first great steps to win control over the world in which he lived had already been taken—the control of fire, the use of the wheel, the domestication of animals and cultivation of crops, weaving and the art of building houses. In fact these already belonged to a remote and primitive past for the great civilizations which, about 4000 BC, grew up in the valley of the Nile and in Mesopotamia. The Pyramids were already old; and Mesopotamia was dotted with cities of great wealth and culture, each an independent state and already skilled in the game of power politics.[1]

In spite of all the changes of fortune involved in this game, there is a certain stability about the situation in Mesopotamia in the third millennium. But about 2000 BC the established order

[1] This period in history is not really our concern; but besides being interesting in itself, some knowledge of it helps to give a proper perspective to the Bible. See, then, V. Gordon Childe, *What Happened in History*, Pelican ed. (1946); Kathleen M. Kenyon, *Digging up Jericho* (1957).

of things seems to crumble, the clear pattern breaks up in confusion; and for a period the picture is obscured by shifting masses of people who have left so little mark on history that even their names sound strange to us.

There are, for example, the Hurrians—a people of mixed race from somewhere near the Caspian Sea, who, with chariots and a new type of bow, swept down into Mesopotamia and Syria. By the fifteenth century such a city as Nuzi, on the upper reaches of the Tigris, was almost completely Hurrian; and a little later they had even carved out a kingdom for themselves in northern Mesopotamia, the kingdom of Mitanni. Further south, too, their influence was so strongly felt that the Egyptians in the fourteenth century could refer to the country north of Egypt's borders as "the land of the Hurrians".[2]

But an even greater threat to the civilization of Mesopotamia was the pressure of the semi-nomadic peoples who were roaming on the edges of the desert but who were continually attracted by the comfort and wealth of the more settled districts. One such group was known as the "Amorites" (the name simply means "the Westerners"). Their invasion took the form not

[2] These people appear in the Bible as the "Horites" (e.g., Deut. 2.12) and even as "Hivites" (Exod. 3.8).

of massed attack but of gradual infiltration followed by local struggles for power; but by this process most of the city states of Mesopotamia fell under Amorite control. These newcomers from the desert did not forge new patterns of society for themselves, but adopted the ways of their predecessors—including the system of independent city states competing for superiority. By about 1800 BC, one of them, Babylon, achieved such a position of authority as to form a Babylonian Empire. The best-known ruler of this empire is Hammurabi, whose name is associated with that collection and arrangement of laws which is known as "the Code of Hammurabi".

Westwards too the Amorites were on the move, following the same process of infiltration into the land of Canaan. This territory was nominally under Egyptian dominion; but in practice their control did not extend beyond the coastal plain; inland, the semi-nomadic peoples roamed at will and gradually settled down in independent cities.[3] In fact, Egypt herself was soon under pressure from this wave of new peoples from the

[3] Valuable information about this period is given by the *Tale of Sinuhe*, an Egyptian exile's account of life in Canaan (*ANET*, 18–22); and the "Execration Texts" —Egyptian texts expressing curses on their enemies, giving us incidentally information about these enemies. (*ANET*, 328–9.)

north; and about 1750 she succumbed to this pressure and came under the dominion of rulers whom she called the Hyksos, "foreign princes".

## 2. THE PATRIARCHS IN THEIR WORLD

At first sight, the picture thus presented is very different from the world of the Patriarchs as presented in the Bible: on the one hand, peoples and tribes, on the other, one man and his family.

But we have already seen that popular tradition, such as we have in this part of the Bible, deals with individuals rather than with groups. Moreover, the "popular ethnology" which is characteristic of this type of narrative often uses the individuals as representatives of the whole group; tribal or national relationships are expressed in terms of family relationships. (See pp. 5f.) The story of the Patriarchs is best understood in the light of this principle. History and archaeology can only speak in vague and general terms of "population shifts"; out of this faceless, nameless mass, the Bible brings to light Abraham, Isaac and Jacob. This does not mean that Abraham, Isaac and Jacob are not real people; but it does mean that they stand also for the larger groups which they represent. Under the apparent simplicity of the story of a family we are to see something of the history of the peoples from which Israel was formed.

Israel's ancestors, then, were semi-nomadic wanderers from Mesopotamia, part of the Amorite infiltration into Canaan in the early part of the second millennium. There they continued their pastoral way of life; their possessions were sheep and goats; they were concerned with wells and water supplies; they never wandered far into the desert, and were usually close to some town like Hebron where they could buy corn or the ornaments which Abraham's servants took to Rebekah. Gradually they adopted some of the customs of sedentary life; larger animals like oxen were added to their possessions (Gen. 32.15), and there are even references to agriculture in the story of Joseph (the dream of the sheaves of corn, Gen. 37.5–7).

Many an incident in the history of the Patriarchs is illuminated by recent discoveries of the customs of the time.[4] To mention only two: The little incident concerning Rachel's theft of her father's "household gods" (Gen. 31.19–35) seems like a great fuss over very little; until we

[4] Cf. R. T. O'Callaghan, "Historical Parallels to Patriarchal Customs", *Catholic Biblical Quarterly* (1944), 391–405. This is one of the subjects on which archaeological research has been most fruitful, and further examples can be found in most popular works on biblical archaeology.

find that possession of these objects guaranteed
a claim to inheritance of the family property.
Again, it is rather puzzling to find that when
Abraham tries to buy some land for a family
burial ground (Gen. 23.1–18), the owner tries to
get him to take the whole field; but this too
becomes clear when we realize that the possession of a field carries with it feudal duties—and
the owner is trying to hand these on to Abraham.

We know in general, then, the world to which
the Patriarchs belong. Can we determine Israel's
origins more precisely? This is very difficult, because they probably included several different
groups of people of different races. "Your father
was an Amorite and your mother a Hittite", says
Ezekiel (16.3); and though this is intended as a
jibe—and certainly as far as the Hittites were
concerned is completely untrue—nevertheless
it does suggest that Israel recognized that her
ancestry was very complex. It is remarkable that
many of the parallels to the patriarchal history—
including the two examples given above—come
to us from the Hurrian city of Nuzi already
referred to. This might imply that there was a
strong Hurrian strain in Israel's stock. But on
the other hand it is possible that the Hurrians
maintained the customs of the Amorites from
whom they captured the city. Israel also recognized her kinship with the Arameans: "A

wandering Aramean was my father..." (Deut. 26.5.) This is confirmed by the name of the district where Abraham's relatives lived, Aram Naharaim or Paddan-Aram. The story of Jacob in particular shows close relationship with this district—his mother Rebekah came from there, it was there that he himself went to seek a wife, and Laban, his father-in-law, is explicitly called an Aramean.

The Arameans, however, are an offshoot of the Amorites. We may reconstruct the situation, then, like this. The wave of migration which broke over the Near East in the first half of the second millennium was predominantly Amorite. Some of these settled down in Mesopotamia, and were later known as the Arameans. Others made their way to Canaan, where they were followed by other peoples, such as the Hurrians, with whom they sometimes became inseparably mixed; but from time to time they continued to receive fresh reinforcements from the Aramean branch of the family. And the patriarchal history preserves the memory of these events in the traditions concerning Abraham, Isaac and Jacob.

### 3. THE RELIGION OF THE PATRIARCHS

But the Bible does not preserve these traditions for their historical interest or out of family pride. They are preserved because Israel saw in them a certain religious importance. Here, too, however, we must attempt to see first the historical situation.

The Bible itself reminds us that Abraham's ancestors adored "false gods". (Cf. Joshua 24.2.) This was no doubt the worship of the moon, which was practised at both Ur and Haran; and it is probably significant that the name of Abraham's father, Terah, means "moon".

In Canaan, they seem to have adapted themselves to the form of worship prevalent there. The most striking characteristic of this religion, to a modern reader, is the way in which religion pervaded the whole of existence. It is not merely that every aspect of life, every important moment, had its appropriate religious ceremonial; the two spheres, the religious and the secular, actually seemed to overlap. This is mainly due to men's view of the world at that time. The world of ancient man (and indeed of men right up to relatively modern times) was a strange and frightening place. All sorts of things took place which men could come to recognize and even anticipate, but which they could neither explain nor control. This was true not only of rare or extraordinary events like eclipses or earthquakes, but even of such ordinary things as the alternation of the seasons or the growth

of the crops. Today we have a "scientific" explanation of these things; but without such an
explanation, the world would indeed be a
haunted garden. To them it was a haunted
garden populated and controlled by invisible
beings, the "gods".

But although the gods were so close to men,
they were still greater, more powerful, superior;
and this attitude is, so to speak, "localized" by
representing the gods as dwelling on a mountain-
top. This mountain, moreover, was situated in
some inaccessible, remote place—just as the gods
themselves were constantly involved in human
life but always beyond the range of man's per-
ception. In Greek mythology we are familiar
with Mount Olympus as the home of the gods;
and similarly in Semitic thought the gods were
situated on "the mountains of the north". (Cf.
Ps. 47.3.) The same trend of thought led the
Babylonians to build their temples in the form
of terraced towers called *ziggurats*—a sort of
artificial mountain at the top of which the god
dwelt. Similarly mountains or "high places" were
favourite places for the worship of the god, and
these places were surrounded by the awe, the
terror, that attached to the god itself. Thus the
people were warned not to set foot on Mount
Sinai, "the holy mountain", in case they should

be destroyed by the aura of power which emanated from God.[5]

The same atmosphere of religious awe attached to other places connected with the god—trees, streams, caverns. Such a place was designated as sacred by the reputed appearance of the god in it, or it would be made known to some believer in a dream. .

These ideas were shared by the Patriarchs. Abraham raised an altar to God at the oak of Moreh (Gen. 12.6–7), near the oak of Mamre (Gen. 13.18), and at the well of Beersheba he planted a tamarisk tree and invoked "El Olam" (Gen. 21.33). That name—"God the Everlasting"—is the Canaanite title of one of their gods, as also are the other names which Abraham used: "El Elyon", God Most High (Gen. 14.22), "El Shaddai", God of the Mountains (Gen. 17.1).

Abraham was joined to his God in a "covenant". This too is a feature which is found in contemporary religion, and it is best understood against the background of semi-nomadic society. In such a society, the family is the essential element, far more evidently than it is in a civilization of towns or cities. The family—or its extension, the clan or tribe—provides the support and protection which people need from

[5] Cf. R. Otto, *The Idea of the Holy*, Pelican ed. (1959).

society. Abraham going unhesitatingly to the support of Lot, in Genesis 14, is a typical example of the way this system would work. If a man were attacked, his kinsmen rallied to his support; if he were killed, they would avenge his death. This is called acting as *go'el*, a word which in English is often translated as "redeemer".

This relationship depended on ties of blood. But it could be supplemented by an agreement or alliance between two clans who were not related by blood, but whose alliance was looked on as forming a bond equivalent to blood-relationship. This was the covenant.

A comparison between Genesis 13.5–11 and 21.25–7 is instructive. In both cases the situation is the same: two groups, those of Abraham and Lot in the first case and Abraham and Abimelech in the second, have become so numerous that a dispute rises over water supplies; in both cases the parties come to an agreement; but in the case of Abraham and Abimelech a covenant is made, while there is no such mention of an alliance between Abraham and Lot. The implication is that there was no need for a covenant between Abraham and Lot since they were kinsmen; but that the covenant between Abraham and Abimelech was looked on as constituting a bond equivalent to blood-relationship.

This relationship could also exist between a man and his god. This is evidenced from proper names of the time; Eliab, for example, meaning, "My god is a father to me"; or Abimelech, meaning, "My father is Melech." And it was this relationship which God entered into with Abraham. From now on, their interests are inseparably linked. God becomes the *go'el* of Abraham—his kinsman, bound to come to his assistance. From him Abraham could expect help and all the blessings dear to the heart of a semi-nomad—fertile land and children. But God was still the Almighty; he could not be bound as men are bound; and therefore his part of the Covenant took the form of a promise. And Abraham's part of the Covenant was "faith"— loyalty, trust and unswerving obedience.

Israel's ancestors, then, joined with their God by the bonds of covenant, worshipped him in the only way they knew. Even the moral standards God demanded of them were not strikingly different from those of their contemporaries.[6] But this was the beginning of a journey which was to have an undreamed-of goal. We have seen that

[6] On the whole question of Old-Testament morality, which often seems to be a difficulty, one may see L. Johnston, *Witnesses to God*, 62–74. The same book also gives another view of the story of Abraham, from a more purely religious point of view, 31–41.

the story of their wanderings reads almost like the account of a pilgrimage—a journey from one place to another made holy by God's presence. A pilgrimage indeed it was, a journey in search of the Living God, a journey undertaken in faith. This faith Abraham handed on to his descendants, and blazed a trail for succeeding generations to follow.

# 3

# THE BIRTH OF THE NATION

THE story of the Patriarchs closes with another migration, this time to Egypt. Reduced to essentials, the next stage of the biblical narrative would read something like this.

One of Jacob's sons, Joseph, was taken to Egypt as a slave, but rose to a position of influence and brought the rest of his family to settle there. For a time all went well. The immigrants received favourable treatment and settled in Goshen, north-east of the Nile Delta. But eventually there "rose a king who knew not Joseph", and the privileged position was exchanged for one of slavery.

One of the slaves, Moses, had received his education from the Egyptians but he still felt sufficient sympathy with his own people to strike a blow in their defence. As a result of this he was forced to take refuge in the desert to the east of Egypt, where he was adopted by one of the tribes who wandered there. With them he lived for some time, until he received a call from

God, imposing on him the task of liberating his fellow slaves.

He then returned and extracted from Pharao an agreement to free the slaves, and led them into the desert to Mount Sinai. And it was there that the People of God came into being.

## 1. EGYPT, 1550–1200

Before discussing this period, it will be useful once more to see something of the wider background of the world at that time.

We last saw Egypt helpless under the dominion of foreign rulers, the Hyksos. Their rule lasted about 150 years. Not much is known of this period; the Egyptians did their best to erase the memory of this unhappy interlude in their history, and the Hyksos themselves seem to have indulged in destruction more than in raising monuments. An inscription of Queen Hatshepsut (the only woman "Pharao") reads:

I have restored that which was ruins,
I have raised up that which was unfinished
Since the Asiatics were in Avaris of the north,
And the barbarians in the midst of them.[1]

Avaris, in the north of Egypt, was the Hyksos capital. But at Thebes, the old capital of Egypt,

[1] Cf. *ANET*, 231.

members of the old Egyptian ruling class began
to rouse the country against the usurpers. It was
one of this family, Ahmes, who captured Avaris
and drove the Hyksos out and pursued them
northwards. Then began a series of great military campaigns fired at least partly by a fanatical
hatred of the Hyksos and a determination that
no invader should approach their land again.
The greatest of these military Pharaos was
Thothmes III (1468–1436); in sixteen campaigns
in eighteen summers he pushed Egyptian conquests up as far as the Euphrates (returning each
autumn to adorn the walls of the temple at
Karnak with accounts of his victories).

There, however, the Egyptians came into contact with the Mitanni, the recently founded Hurrian state. To the east, moreover, lay the Hittites,
just beginning to make tentative sorties from their
mountain fastness in Asia Minor. At the moment
they were not strong enough to challenge either
Mitanni or Egypt; but they were a potential
source of danger, a threat sufficient to make both
of them willing to come to terms rather than
to blows. The Egyptian Pharao consented to
receive a Mitanni princess as bride for his son,
and settled down to exploit the vast empire he
had won.

On the next few years we are exceptionally
well informed through the lucky chance of the

discovery of a collection of clay tablets at Tell el-Amarna. These are the foreign-office archives of the time—letters to the Egyptian court from Egypt's dependencies in Canaan, Mitanni and even Babylon.

During the reign of Amenophis III (1406–1370), the tone of the letters points to a stable and firm control. But in the reign of his successor, Amenophis IV (1370–1351), there are evident signs of loss of control: taxes are evaded, local rulers quarrel amongst themselves, the letters are full of charges and counter-charges and suspicious protestations of loyalty. An interesting illustration (particularly in the reference to the *habiru*, as we shall see later) is found in a letter from the ruler of Jerusalem, Abdi-Hiba:

> Verily, this land of Urusalim, neither my father nor my mother has given it to me; the mighty hand of the king gave it to me ... Verily the king has set his name upon the land of Urusalim for ever. Therefore he cannot abandon the lands of Urusalim. Let the king care for his land. The land of the king will be lost. All of it will be taken away from me. There is hostility to me ... But now the *habiru* are taking the cities of the king ... If there are no archers this year, then let the

king send a deputy that he may take me to himself . . . to die with the king, our lord.[2]

The explanation of this deterioration in political conditions is to be found in the actions of the new king. Amenophis IV is sometimes described as the first true monotheist in history; and it is certainly true that he was more interested in religious matters than in affairs of state. The traditional religion of Egypt was polytheist, although in practice the god Amen-Ra had advanced to a position of superiority over the other gods. The king now tried to complete this process by introducing a true monotheism. His chosen god was Aten, the solar disk; and in token of his devotion he himself took a new name, Akhenaten. Not unnaturally, this new religion did not find favour with the official priesthood which surrounded the throne; so the king moved his capital from Thebes to Amarna.

From his time, and possibly from his hand, comes a hymn to the Sun which has some striking similarities to the biblical Psalm 104:

Thou appearest beautifully on the horizon of
    heaven,
Thou living Aten, the beginning of life!
When thou art rising on the eastern horizon
Thou fillest every land with thy beauty.

[2] Cf. *ANET*, 488.

Thou art gracious, great, shining high over
    every land . . .

When thou settest in the western horizon

The land is in darkness in the manner of
    death . . .

Every lion is come forth from his den;

All creeping things, they sting.

Darkness is a shroud and the earth is in still-
    ness

For he who made them rests in his horizon . . .

When thou shinest as the Aten by day,

Thou drivest away the darkness and givest
    thy rays . . .

All the world, they do their work.

How manifold it is, what thou hast made!

They are hidden from the face of man.

O sole god, like whom there is no other!

Thou didst create the world according to thy
    desire

Whilst thou wert alone.

Thou settest every man in his place;

Thou suppliest their needs;

Each has his food, and his time of life is
    reckoned . . .

How effective they are, thy plans, O lord of
    eternity!

Thou makest the seasons in order to rear all
    thou hast made,

The winter to cool them, the heat that they
    may taste thee.
Thou hast made millions of forms of thyself
    alone . . .
For thou art the Aten of the day over the
    earth:
And thou art in my heart.[3]

This impressive religious revolution, however, was short-lived; it died with the king himself. Religious conservatism—and probably
religious self-interest too, embodied in the official
priesthood—were too strong; and Akhenaten's
immediate successor took the name of Tutan-
khamun, in which the reappearance of the
Amun, name of the old god, is significant.

But there was probably political opposition to
Akhenaten also, and with more reason. For in the
Anatolian plain, protected by the barrier of the
Taurus Mountains, a people known as the Hittites had been steadily growing in strength, and
were tempted to emerge from their stronghold
by the wealth of the surrounding civilizations.[4]
Their first efforts at expansion were checked by
the strength of the Mitanni, by the Egyptians and
most of all by their own internal dissensions. But

[3] Cf. *ANET*, 370–71.
[4] On the Hittites, cf. O. R. Gurney, *The Hittites*,
Pelican (1952).

now, about 1380, a ruler named Suppiluliumas showed himself strong enough to impose control on all the factions within the state; and his appearance coincided with the period of weakness in Egypt during the reign of Akhenaten. With this threat removed, Suppiluliumas was able to concentrate on Mitanni. By a daring manoeuvre (crossing the Euphrates and attacking from the rear) he overthrew this kingdom, and followed this up with victorious campaigns against the surrounding minor states. The result was a Hittite empire which had the Lebanon as its southern frontier.

This was too great a danger for Egypt to ignore; and it was probably this which stimulated the reaction against the policy of Akhenaten. Indeed, even under new and more vigorous rulers, Egypt was unable to do more than stem the Hittite advance, not to repulse it. Ramesses II (1302–1234), marching north against them, was ambushed near Kadesh on the Orontes, and only the personal valour of the Pharao saved his army from annihilation. This battle resulted in a treaty of non-aggression, defining the respective spheres of interest of the two powers. Egypt still occasionally waged war in Canaan, feeble gestures of her claim to empire; and it is during one such war, in the reign of Merneptah (1224–1216), that we find the first mention of Israel outside the Bible: Merneptah boasts of his victories: "Canaan is laid waste. . . Israel is destroyed, his seed is not."

But now a new factor appeared on the scene which altered decisively the balance of power. This was the incursion of the "Peoples of the Sea". These were probably peoples from the Aegean Islands, uprooted by the same events as those described in the *Iliad*; there is a certain similarity between their names as recorded by Egyptian monuments and those mentioned by Homer—the Shekelesh (Sicilians), Denyen (Daneans), Luka (Lyceans). They poured over Asia Minor, completely engulfed the Hittite Empire, and ended up at the gates of Egypt. Ramesses III (1195–1164) managed to drive them off, but he could not prevent a group of them—the Pelasata, later known as the Philistines—from landing on the coast of Canaan. This struggle for survival drained Egypt's strength, and set an effective term to her power.

## 2. The Exodus and History

Egyptian records contain no reference to the Exodus; neither do we expect it—the escape of a few slaves would be too small an event to be worth recording, and in any case the Egyptians were not in the habit of recording anything but victories.

Nevertheless, the account given in the Bible fits well into the context we have seen. The story of Joseph is more easily comprehensible if it took place at a time when the rulers of Egypt were Hyksos, Semites themselves like the family of Jacob. When the Hyksos were expelled, the Semites who remained in Egypt would indeed suffer the effects of this change of dynasty. Even the site of the building operations mentioned in the Bible—Ramesses—agrees with information from Egyptian history; Ramesses II, halted in his military exploits by the Hittites, turned his energies instead to raising magnificent buildings; one result of this activity was the rebuilding of the city of Avaris, which was then renamed after Ramesses himself.

The vast Semitic Empire of the Egyptians, with the extensive administration witnessed to by the Amarna tablets, would call for a large civil service; and an obvious source of recruitment for this bureaucracy would be the captives already in Egypt; and it is probable that Moses was one of these. He seems to have been fairly well Egyptianized; even his name has an Egyptian ring; it is from an Egyptian word meaning "to beget", found in such royal names as Thothmes or Tut-moses, meaning "Begotten of the god Thoth."[5]

However, here, as in the history of the Patriarchs, we have to reckon with the possibility and even probability that the Bible is giving a simplification and summary of a much more complex pattern of events. A consideration of the term "Hebrews" gives some indication of what this means. In the Bible, the use of the word is restricted to quite particular circumstances. First of all it is used in Exodus 21.2 (followed by Deut. 15.12 and Jer. 34.9 and 14) in legislation concerning the "Hebrew slaves". Then apart from that it is used only in two groups of texts—those dealing with relationship with the Egyptians, and those dealing with relationship with the Philistines. In other words, it is always used in connection with foreigners (one Israelite never says to another, "I am a Hebrew"), and always when the relationship is one of inferiority.

On the other hand, people known as the *habiru* (the word is variously spelt) are frequently mentioned in non-biblical texts. Placing together these references, we are struck by the immense range of time which they cover, from

[5] The explanation of this name as meaning "taken from the waters" is an example of the "popular etymology" referred to above, p. 5. The story of the child found in a basket by the riverside is also told of the Accadian King Sargon (c. 2300 BC); cf. *ANET*, 119.

the nineteenth to the twelfth centuries; by the astonishing variety of places where they occur, from Mesopotamia to Egypt; and by the surprising variety of roles attributed to these *habiru*—slaves, soldiers, wanderers, city-dwellers and so on. But eventually we are able to make some sort of synthesis of these references and arrive at this understanding of the term: the *habiru* are warlike raiders from the desert, often engaged in pillaging the settled lands or sometimes serving them as mercenaries, and as a result of this often prisoners of war set to work on forced labour. The term, then, is not so much a reference to race or nationality as to social condition.

This does not mean that the Hebrews are to be simply identified with the *habiru*, so that every time we find a reference to these latter we are to apply it to the Israelites. But it does seem clear that the Israelites belong to the same social class as the *habiru*; and this puts the Bible story into a very much wider setting. It was not a unique event for groups of *habiru* to make their way to Egypt; and the sons of Jacob engaged in forced labour would be no different from other groups of *habiru* in the same position.

### 3. THE MEANING OF THE EXODUS

The actual escape from slavery is described for us in terms of religious enthusiasm which over-

shadow the historical event. Overshadow, but
also express the essence of it. For the essential
fact is simply that this event was miraculous; not
in the sense of a crude derogation of the laws of
nature,[6] but in the sense that the deliverance of
these slaves was not due to their own action:
"Not by our strength were we saved, but by the
warrior-force of God." This is the essential factor
which the Bible is intent on conveying and does
in fact convey: that God "with mighty arm and
outstretched hand has set his people free".

Their flight to freedom led them south into
the desert and eventually to Mount Sinai.[7] Here
they encamped for some time; and this period
was an opporunity for reflection and organization
—for reflection on the implications of their
experience, of what had happened to them, and
for working out the organization which suited
this event.

[6] It has long been realized that the "ten plagues" are
natural phenomena—the waters turned into blood, for
example, being a way of describing the thick red sedi-
ment which is occasionally swept down into the Nile
Delta.

[7] Their flight took them first across what the Hebrew
text of the Bible calls the "Yam suph", the "Sea of
Reeds": presumably marshy ground to the north of the
Red Sea proper. The route given next is difficult to
identify, probably because it incorporates two different
traditions; cf. H. Cazelles, *Revue biblique* (1955), 321–
364.

The Bible, too, pauses at this point to insert an account of the social and religious customs which Israel developed in the course of her later history. This expresses her awareness of the fundamental character of this period; here the foundation was laid for all that later Israel was to be; from this ground it grew; this was the moment of birth.

## 1. YAHWEH

We may begin our attempt to understand what the Exodus meant to Israel by a consideration of the name by which they knew their God, the name *Yahweh*.

Yahweh is, so to speak, the proper name of God. A name is not merely a convenient conventional means of specifying a certain individual; it is looked on here as containing the innermost reality of a thing. To know the name is in some way to have a hold on a person, to possess him. To invoke the name is to call the personality into play. "Name", in fact, can be translated almost as "personality". To know the name of God, then, was an immense step forward in relationship with God. The Patriarchs had known God indeed, but only now did the people "know him by name". (Cf. Exod.3.13–15: 6.2–3.)

The origin of this name is unknown.[8] But the Israelites connected it with the verb "to be", and interpreted it as meaning "I am". This is simply an assertion of existence, of reality. The name gives possession of the person; but Yahweh is a God who cannot thus be possessed, in the way that the gods of Egypt, for example, could be possessed by those who knew their names. To say simply that "he is", then, implies that his true being is beyond the grasp of man's mind. But it is enough—and more than enough, a subject for perpetual joy and gratitude—to know that he is; to know the God who really is and who alone really is.

## 2. THE GOD WHO ACTS

This in turn is connected with another indelible mark that the Exodus left on Israel. For it was in the Exodus that they came to know their God, Yahweh. Whenever later Israel sought to explain the basis of their faith, it was not to any

[8] It has been suggested that traces of this name for God have been found outside of Israel, among the Kennites, for example; but the evidence is not convincing. With more probability it is suggested that the element "yau" is added to some Semitic proper names with the meaning "mine"—that is to say, "*my* god". This would agree with the idea of a personal relationship to a god which, we have seen, is a feature of some forms of Semitic religion.

reasoning or proof or argument that they appealed, but to the fact that God had delivered them from Egypt and made them his people.

This involved a totally new concept of divinity, of the nature of the gods. Other gods were nature gods; in some form or other they represented the forces at work in man's environment. But this meant that the gods themselves were bound to the cycle of nature; this is what they are, this is their nature; the sun god is one who progresses through the heavens by day and traverses the dark underworld by night; it is the character and being of the corn god that he dies in winter and comes to life again in spring. But here Israel finds a God who is outside the cycle of nature, outside our world. So far from being bound up with it, he himself directs it with supreme freedom and mastery. The pagan gods cannot break the cycle to which they are bound; they cannot really act, and therefore, as Israelite apologetic delighted in pointing out, they do not really exist: "The idols have feet but cannot walk, they have eyes but cannot see." Therefore they are non-being, emptiness, "vanity". In contrast to gods of such a kind, the God of Israel "is". He is, because he acts; and they know that he is, because they have experienced his action.

But this in turn involves a different conception of human life. If God has thus intervened in events, then human life is the sphere of his activity; not merely indirectly, as with the gods who act in man's environment, but directly, God can and does act in human life. But that means that human life is meaningful and purposeful. It is the beginning of a real concept of history.[9] This is reflected in Israel's great feasts. Originally these were festivals connected with the cycle of nature; the Passover, for example, clearly combines the spring festivals of a pastoral and of an agricultural people, the one concerned with the flock and the other concerned with the corn. But Israel transformed these festivals and made them the occasion for commemorating and renewing the historical facts concerned with their salvation.

### 3. THE GOD OF ISRAEL

But it was not to the wider and more theoretical implications of the Exodus that Israel attended primarily. What was uppermost in their experience was the fact that God had acted for *them*; and this meant that God had chosen them. They were in some special relationship with him. When they were slaves, powerless

[9] On all of this, see G. E. Wright, *God Who Acts* (1952); and see later, in connection with the Prophets, p. 168.

under oppression, he had gratuitously intervened to give them freedom and to bring them to birth as a nation.

Many of the expressions which are most characteristic of Israel's literature can be seen as attempts to formulate this idea of election. For example, they were God's adopted sons (Exod. 4.22); and God was their Father not merely in the general sense of a provident deity, but in the very specific sense that he brought them into being. God cared for them, led them to safety—led them through the desert like a shepherd, and they were the sheep of his pasturing. (Ps. 94.7; 79.1 etc.) In the desert they were nursed by him, like a tree which springs up as from nothing, which, given water, flourishes, and without it dies. (Isa. 5.1–7; Ps. 79.9–19.) God was their king; as a nation they owed their existence to him and their lives were under his control. As with a king, their victories depend on him; they had been freed from captivity, and this was a great victory over the Egyptians, but the victory was none of their doing; God was the victor; God was a warrior who had taken up arms in their defence and would do so again. (Ps. 27.7.) And finally, it gave them the realization of two qualities of God which were always on their lips —his "goodness and truth": his goodness is that love, that mercy, that gratuitous kindness which

was characteristic of one who had found them
worthless slaves and for no motive other than his
own goodness had set them free (Deut. 7.7–8);
and his truth is his reliability, his trustworthi-
ness, which in their own helplessness they had
tested and not found wanting.

## 4. THE COVENANT

All of this, all Israel's relationship with
Yahweh, found its most essential expression in
the Covenant.

The patriarchal covenant, we saw, could be
understood in the light of semi-nomadic customs.
The covenant of Sinai may be based on the form
followed by international agreements of that
time—a treaty between an overlord and a vassal
state.[10] Such treaties begin with the title of the
sovereign and a reminder of the deeds which
have put his vassals under obligation; just as in
the Decalogue, "I am Yahweh your God, who

[10] Cf. G. Mendenhall, *Law and Covenant in Israel and
the Ancient Near East* (1955). Some scholars see no need
for any other explanation of the covenant form than
the experience of the Exodus itself, binding Israel to
God by ties of loyalty and obligation. Nevertheless, the
similarity with the form of suzerainty treaties is striking, as the comparison made in the text shows. Perhaps
one could say that at least this form was used to express
a relationship already realized on other grounds, the
grounds of the Exodus itself.

brought you out of captivity in Egypt." Then the stipulations of the treaty are laid down; among them the obligation to refrain from alliance with any of the king's enemies and of supporting him in time of war; as, in Israel, the injunction "not to have other gods besides me", and the concept of the "war for Yahweh" as we shall see it later. (p. 68.) The treaty ends with a series of blessings and cursings which could be paralleled from those in Leviticus 26.3–43. And finally the treaty is ordered to be read out publicly to the people and a copy of it stored up in the shrine of the god and brought out on occasion to be read to the people to remind them of their obligations—as was done with Israel's law, kept in the Ark and brought out to be read publicly to the people. (Deut. 31.9ff.)

This concept of covenant summed up all that the experience of those days meant to Israel. At the Exodus God had delivered them by an act of gracious mercy and by doing so had chosen them as his own, had made them his own people. He was their God, they were his people. (Exod. 6.7.) His word is their law—and the reverse is equally true; their laws are the expression of his will. The roots of Israel's political and religious organization go back to this period and are the expressions of the truth that God is their ruler. Obviously, this law was not invented *ab ovo.* They had precedents to guide them in the legislation of other peoples of the time, and much of their laws can be paralleled from other ancient legal codes, such as the Code of Hammurabi.[11]

In this legislation, political and religious laws are found side by side. Some of the laws are purely social in character; the laws of cleanliness, for example, are partly hygienic and therefore part of the normal social legislation to be expected in any society; the laws concerning clean and unclean animals, on the other hand, may be the result of a campaign against animals considered sacred in other religions. But all of them together serve to mark out Israel's character as "holy", as different, as set aside for the service of their God. All of these laws enter into Israel's "constitution" as not merely another nation like any other, but as a nation which is the People of God.

The covenant idea is expressed too in the central feature of their religion—the tabernacle enshrining the "Ark of the Covenant". The Ark was a small chest which was understood to be a container for a copy of the Law, or according to another tradition, the throne of God. The two

---

[11] *ANET*, 166–77, gives extracts from the Code of Hammurabi with references showing the frequent points of contact with the laws of the Pentateuch.

concepts are not incompatible;[12] and in either view, the Ark represents God enthroned as their king, and dwelling in their midst in the Tabernacle, "the tent of meeting", the place where they can meet God. Their covenant king is Emmanuel, "God-with-us". The Covenant was sealed by a common meal in one tradition, by the sprinkling of blood in another (Exod. 24.5–9); both signify a union of life between God and the people.

There are certain differences between this type of covenant and the patriarchal covenant. The latter consisted simply of a promise by God, in which Abraham had only to put his faith. The covenant of Sinai was based on God's saving act, which gave rise to an obligation. St Paul, later, was to become acutely aware of the differences involved in these two concepts. Nevertheless, Israel itself was conscious of the continuity between the two; God showed himself to Moses from the very beginning as "the God of Abraham, Isaac and Jacob" (Exod. 3.6); and though he had not revealed his "name" to these ancestors, he was still the same God, dealing with them in the same way. (Exod. 6.3–4.) The differences, therefore, must not be exaggerated; as St Paul himself realized, the second covenant does not annul the first (Gal. 3.17), and underlying the

[12] Cf. R. de Vaux, *Ancient Israel*, 297–302.

differences there is a basic unity. The covenant with the Patriarchs involved a promise on God's part and faith on man's; but in the covenant of Sinai, too, promise and faith are involved. The promise is not yet explicit, but it is involved in the very idea of election; if God has chosen them, he has chosen them for some purpose; if God is with them, then under his guidance and protection they can expect further deeds of mercy. And for Israel as for Abraham, this election called for faith and loyalty, of which their obedience to the covenant law is merely the external sign.

## 5. THE PEOPLE OF ISRAEL

The experiences surrounding the Exodus, summed up in the Covenant, determined Israel's national way of life. But the Covenant did even more; in a certain sense it even determined their national existence. It is not merely that there was a nation called Israel which the Covenant formed into a certain type of nation; it is even true that the Covenant *makes* them into a nation.

The Bible consistently represents Israel as descended from Jacob through his twelve sons. Jacob is even provided with an alternative name which is that of the nation descended from him,

THE BIRTH OF THE NATION

"Israel" (Gen. 32.28f), implying that in him the whole nation is potentially contained; and equally, the nation itself is known as "the sons of Jacob".

However, one can sense a certain artificiality in this representation. For one thing, the number twelve is only obtained by allotting two of the tribes, Ephraim and Manasseh, to Jacob's grandsons, not to his sons (Gen. 48.8ff); of "the twelve", Simeon plays no part in the later history, Levi plays no political part, and Reuben hardly any part; moreover, in an early account of the action of the tribes (Judges 5.14–17), not all the names of Jacob's sons are represented, but two others, Machir and Gilead, are mentioned. In other words, we have every reason to think that the picture of the nation of Israel being formed by simple physical descent from Jacob's twelve sons is a simplified and conventional picture.

Moreover, the Bible goes to some trouble to explain to us the precise paternity—or to be more precise, maternity—of these twelve sons. They are all begotten of Jacob, but are begotten by four different mothers; Reuben, Simeon, Levi and Judah are born first to Leah; then Dan and Naphtali to Rachel's maidservant Bilhah; then Leah's servant Zilpah bears Gad and Asher; then Leah again gives birth to Issachar and Zebulun; and finally Rachel herself bears Joseph and Benjamin. Now we have already remarked the technique by which the Bible portrays the history of the group through the history of its ancestors. Therefore it seems probable that this complicated account of Jacob's "twelve sons" is intended to indicate to us the fact that the twelve tribes of Israel stood in varying degrees of relationship to each other.

Moreover, the Bible itself says that the people who came out of Egypt were "a motley group". (Exod. 12.38; Num. 11.4.) There were Egyptians among them (cf. Lev. 24.10), Midianites (Num. 10.29–32), and Kennizites joined them shortly afterwards (Joshua 14.13–14); and of course in the process of settling into Canaan later many other racial elements were absorbed into the nation.

We have already noted that one clan or tribe could be linked with another by covenant in a relationship which was the equivalent of blood-kinship (cf. p. 23), and when this happened it was a quite normal convention to express this in a genealogy tracing them back to a common ancestor. We have actual textual evidence of this process in the Bible itself. In a text just referred to, Joshua 14.14, Caleb is referred to as a Kennizite; but he links his fortune with the sons of Jacob, therefore in Num. 13.7 he is said to be "of the tribe of Judah"; and by 1 Chron. 2.8–18 he has a regular place in the genealogy of Judah. This was hardly a unique and isolated instance. This was the way in which all this "motley group" came to be "Israel", the confederation of the tribes known as "the sons of Jacob".

And the Covenant which brought about this confederation was the Covenant of Sinai. There the link was forged which bound together these different groups into one. Without the Covenant, we have only a disparate collection of runaway slaves. With it, we have the nation of Israel.

# 4

# SETTLEMENT IN CANAAN

T HE new people which had come into existence in the desert of Arabia were in the nature of the case semi-nomadic; their livelihood depended on the flocks which they led in search of the scanty pasture. By an evolution quite natural to such peoples—we have seen it earlier in the case of the Amorites—the time came when the attraction of the richer lands drew them to exchange their wandering state for a settled life. The nearest territory suitable for this purpose was the land of Canaan.

## 1. THE LAND OF CANAAN

This tiny strip of land between the desert and the sea was indeed a land flowing with milk and honey for the tribes from the harsh and barren land around. It was "a good land, a land of streams of water, of fountains and springs flowing forth from valley and hill; a land of wheat and barley, of vines and fig trees and pomegranates, a land of olive trees and honey" (Deut. 8.7–8); and even the Egyptian Sinuhe describes it as "a good land. Figs were in it and grapes. It had more wine than water. Plentiful was its honey, abundant its olives."[1]

Geographically, the most striking feature of this land is the "ditch" formed by the Jordan, supplied by springs from Lebanon and Hermon, flowing through Lake Huleh and the Sea of Galilee down to the Dead Sea. The climate of this valley, in which the Jordan twists and turns bewilderingly, is practically tropical. On either side the land rises steeply to a mountain range which on the west forms a spine running north and south. This in turn falls away to the low-lands (the Shephelah) of the west, which lead to the fertile coastal strip; and in the south to the Negeb, desert land which, however, with careful irrigation can be made to support a good population.

East of the Jordan valley the land was occupied by peoples of Amorite stock, descendants of the semi-nomadic migrants referred to earlier. There were the Moabites east of the Dead Sea, with their northern border usually on the river Arnon; and south of these the Edomites. Both of these had adopted sedentary life and monarchic government in the thirteenth century, just before the arrival of the sons of Israel. North of these were the Ammonites, still semi-

[1] *ANET*, 19.

nomadic at this time but sedentarized shortly
afterwards; and north of these again were Aramean tribes.[2]

But it was the favoured climate of the land
west of the Jordan which made it particularly
attractive to peoples in search of a home. It had
already been the scene of many such immigra-
tions prior to that of the Israelites. There were
the Amorites and Hurrians of whom we have
already spoken (p. 14); and the Bible speaks
of Hittites also.[3] But by the thirteenth century,
all these elements had been moulded into a
single unity to which the term "Canaanite"
could properly be applied; with one language
(though with variations of dialect), one type of
religion, and one culture.

[2] All of these belong to the same general north-
western Semitic group of peoples as Israel, and the
Israelites recognized this kinship. The Moabites and
Ammonites are said to be descended from Abraham's
nephew Lot (Gen. 19.37–8); and the Edomites are
descended from Jacob's brother Esau (cf. Gen. 25.30:
26.9; and much of the story of Esau clearly refers rather
to the Edomite people than to the individual Esau).
For the Arameans, connected with Israel through Jacob,
see pp. 19 and 143.

[3] These Hittites are mentioned particularly in connection with Hebron, Gen. 23.2ff. But the great Hittite
Empire never extended as far south as this. Either these
Hittites, then, were individual immigrants, or the Bible
is using the term loosely to indicate people from the
same general region of Asia Minor from which the
Hittites also came.

This culture was a very real achievement, as the excavations at Ugarit (modern Ras-Shamra) show. Not the least remarkable of its features was the amazing versatility of the scribes, who were able to write several different languages in a variety of scripts—including an alphabetic script which is the ancestor of our own alphabet. But it is the contents of their writings which are most revealing. For this is the style and language which is nearest to that in which the early Israelites spoke and wrote; and here for the first time we have direct evidence of the thoughts and mentality of the people with whom Israel had closest contact and kinship.

In particular, these myths and legends give us clear information about the religion of Canaan. This was essentially a fertility cult, preoccupied with the problem of ensuring fertility for men, animals and crops. Nominally the chief god was El; but in practice a greater part was played by his son Baal; and with him are associated the goddesses Asherah, Astarte (found in the plural in the Bible, Ashteroth), and Anat. Baal (meaning "lord", or "husband") was originally the title of the storm god; but in Canaan he had come to be the god of the crops; and it was in this role that the myth of his death and resurrection was enacted, in order to ensure the death and resurrection of the crops. Since the life and strength of mankind was considered to be closely linked with that of nature, this form of religion also involved such practices as sacred prostitution.

Politically, the unity of Canaan was less evident—except insofar as there was a unified pattern of disunity. The social organization of the country was one of "city states", each with its own "king". The bulk of the population engaged in agriculture round some strongly walled town, and looked to the city and its king for protection and refuge in times of trouble. Besides being farmers, the Canaanites were great traders, exporting timber and dyed textiles,[4] and importing pottery from as far away as Crete; and the wealth that trade brings has left its mark on the cities, which often have well-built houses, elaborate arrangements of tunnels and wells to ensure the ever-important water supply,[5] and a good drainage system.

Such a form of social organization made any kind of coherent national policy impossible and led to dispersion of effort. At various times the

[4] The name "Canaan", like Phoenicia in Greek, is taken from the word "purple", referring to the purple dye for which the country was famous.

[5] Excavations at el-Jib, ancient Gibeon, have brought to light an excellent example of a Canaanite water system; cf. J. B. Pritchard, *Gibeon, Where the Sun Stood Still* (1962), 53–78.

country came within the sphere of interest of one or other of the great powers, Egypt or Mesopotamia, especially the former; and at such periods the authority of the ruling power imposed a certain unity on the country. But in the thirteenth century Egyptian power was exhausted by the Peoples of the Sea, and the only remaining great power in Mesopotamia was Assyria, which was not yet strong enough to entertain imperial designs. The result was a vacuum of power which was the opportunity for smaller nations such as Israel to make their way.

## 2. Joshua and Judges

The biblical account of Israel's occupation of Canaan is given in the books of Joshua and Judges. But in order to assess correctly the information given in these books we must first take note of their literary formation. These books form part of the great Deuteronomic history which runs from Deuteronomy to Kings. This collection is marked by concern for the characteristic teachings of the Book of Deuteronomy—the doctrine of election, the obligations of the Covenant, the connection between Israel's fulfilment of her obligations and her success or failure. The following passage is typical of the Deuteronomist:

3

If Yahweh has chosen you, it is not because you are more numerous than any other nation; for indeed you are less than any people; but it is because he has loved you ... Know then that Yahweh your God is the true God, the faithful God who keeps his covenant and his love through generation after generation for those who love him and and keep his commands, but who punishes those who hate him ... If you listen to his commands and hold fast to them and put them into practice, Yahweh your God will keep the covenant and the faithful love which he swore to your fathers. He will love you, bless you, make you great; he will bless your offspring and your land ... You will eat up all those nations which Yahweh your God has delivered to you ... He will hand kings over to your power and you will wipe out the memory of their name. (Deut. 7.7–24.)

This is the thesis of which the history which follows is a concrete illustration. The Book of Joshua, for example, begins with these words of God to Joshua: "You are the one who will put the people in possession of the land which I swore to their fathers that I would give them. Have courage, stand firm, take care to act according to the Law ... Let the book of this Law be always on your lips; ponder it day and night ...

then you will be successful." (Joshua 1.2–8.) And summing up again at the end, Joshua says: "You are witnesses of what Yahweh your God has done for you to all these nations; Yahweh your God has fought for you . . . and the people who are still to be conquered, Yahweh your God will send them fleeing before you . . . You will take care, upon your lives, to love Yahweh your God. But if you turn away, know then that Yahweh will cease to set the nations fleeing before you, and they will become a trap and a snare for you." (Joshua 23.3–13.) And even more explicitly in Judges, a prologue sets this theological tone for the book which follows: "Then the children of Israel did what was displeasing to Yahweh and served Baals . . . Then the anger of Yahweh blazed out against Israel and he delivered them into the hands of brigands who despoiled them and into the hands of the enemies who surrounded them, and they were not able to resist . . . Then God sent them Judges; Yahweh was with the Judge, and he saved them from their foes while the Judge lived, for Yahweh allowed himself to be moved to pity when they groaned beneath the yoke of their oppressors; but once the Judge was dead they fell away again . . ." (Judges 2.11–19.)

But this pattern, this theological thesis, is presented through materials already existing.

This material is extremely varied in character. In the Book of Joshua, for example, we are struck by the contrast between the detailed, repetitive account of the first stages of the penetration (chapters two to seven—six chapters to cover about twenty miles), and the extremely laconic, schematic account of the conquest of the whole of the rest of the country (Chapter 10 for the whole of the south, Chapter 11 for the whole of the north). It has been suggested that these early chapters were a local Benjaminite tradition conserved at the shrine of Gilgal, which plays such a great part in these chapters; while for the rest of the history the editor has at his disposal essentially only the account of two battles, one in the south and the other in the north, to which he has attached the complete conquest of south and north respectively. The division of the conquered land which follows, it has been suggested, is drawn principally from administrative documents of the time of the monarchy. But what is in any case clear is that this material did not form originally a "History of the Conquest", but that this form has been imposed on it by a later editor.

The origin of the Book of Judges is even clearer. Substantially the book consists of an account of six "heroes" of Israel, whose exploits are precisely such as would be treasured by the tribes to which they belonged. These tribal, local traditions were then gathered together, and to them were added six other names to make up the number twelve corresponding to the traditional number of the tribes of Israel.

### 3. THE INVASION

With this account of the literary character of the books in mind, we may now consider their historical character. The general impression given by Joshua is of a swift, successful invasion of Canaan by the whole people under the single leadership of Joshua. This impression, however, is modified by occasional texts which admit that it was not quite as simple as this: certain parts of the country remain unconquered (13.1–7: 17.12–18); the tribe of Dan is ousted from its original settlement (19.47); the independent action of certain groups is admitted (14.6–13: 15.13–19). And this modification of the first impression is reinforced by the first chapter of the Book of Judges. This begins as if it were a continuation of Joshua, with Judah appointed as leader of the nation in succession to Joshua, as Joshua was the successor to Moses; but it immediately becomes clear that "Judah" now stands not for an individual but for the tribe. The text then goes on to describe the exploits

of this tribe, associated now with the tribe of
Simeon and the allied clan of the Kennites; and
to them are attributed victories already attributed to the whole people under Joshua. The
general impression given in this book, then, is
that the conquest was a slow, laborious infiltration of several tribes acting more or less independently. This latter picture is the one we
should expect: the terrain was difficult; the
mountainous country in which the invaders
would find themselves almost immediately after
crossing the Jordan was much more suited to
small local action than to the combined
manœuvres of large bodies of men; the Canaanite
towns were strongly fortified, and as both Joshua
and Judges point out (Joshua 17.16; Judges 1.19),
the newcomers had no weapons to match the
Canaanite chariots.

It appears, then, that the Book of Joshua is a
summary version of something which was in fact
much more complicated; this summary was
adequate for the editor's purpose of showing the
victory of God's people under God's leadership,
but it was not intended to be a complete account
of the period. (One may compare this to what we
have already seen of the position of Moses in
regard to the Pentateuch: laws and customs
which developed slowly over a fairly long period
of time are here summarily attributed to Moses;

and in the same way the whole conquest, a lengthy and difficult process, is attributed to Joshua.)

There is even reason to think that the matter is more complicated yet. The full account of these arguments cannot be gone into here[6]; but to give some idea of what they are, we may consider certain peculiarities in the narrative as we have it in the Bible. We have already seen (p. 49) that the relationship between the twelve sons of Jacob is intended to express the relationship between the tribes which these sons represent. Reuben, Simeon and Levi are the three eldest brothers, which should indicate that these were three of the most important tribes. Yet in the history as we have it in the Bible, Reuben plays a very minor part, Simeon practically no part at all, and Levi becomes a purely religious organization with no part in the political and military activity of the tribes. The claim of these tribes to priority, then, must rest on their importance in the period before the invasion. But this can hardly be true in Egypt; therefore it was presumably in Canaan.

[6] For a complete account of the complex situation showing the many factors of many different kinds—literary, historical, archaeological—which have to be taken into account, see H. H. Rowley, *From Joseph to Joshua* (1950).

This in turn leads us to take a second look at the references to the *habiru* in non-biblical documents. These *habiru* are not simply to be identified with the Hebrews, but certainly the Hebrews seem to belong to the same category of persons as that described by the word *habiru*. (Cf. p. 37.) But the Tell el-Amarna letters of the fourteenth century—prior to the Exodus, that is—mention the *habiru* as then being active in Canaan.

They even mention them specifically in connection with Shechem.[7] It is probably going beyond our present evidence to connect this in turn with the incident related in Genesis 34, where Simeon and Levi are responsible for an attack on Shechem; but at least this incident does illustrate the way the Hebrews would appear to the people of those days—as untrustworthy, violent brigands; in other words, very much like the *habiru* of the profane documents.

The reference to Shechem is particularly interesting, however, for another reason. In Joshua's account of the conquest of Canaan, the first few stages are described in detail, then the conquest of the south is described, and then the conquest of the north; but there is no account of the conquest of the centre of the country, round Shechem. And yet this district is later

[7] Cf. *ANET*, 486.

found to be so firmly in Israelite hands that it can be chosen as their first tribal meeting-place. (Joshua 24.) This would certainly be more comprehensible if it were already in the hands of tribes with whom the invaders could claim some kinship—tribes like Reuben, Simeon and Levi, for example.

In a word, then, it would seem that the best explanation of much of the evidence—and the best solution to many of the difficulties—is that "the sons of Israel" are a confederation of various groups who have undergone quite a varied history; not all of them went down to Egypt, and of those who did, some of them may have returned earlier than, and independently of, the main group led by Joshua.

On the other hand, to dismiss the Book of Joshua as a complete idealization is going too far. There is archaeological evidence to show that several of the towns mentioned among Joshua's conquests were in fact destroyed violently in the late thirteenth century. This is true of Bethel, Debir, Lachish and Hazor; and in the case of the last two, the period of occupation following the destruction is much poorer—as would be expected of invaders from the desert new to civilization.

We may conclude, then, that the Israelites did enter Canaan by force in the late thirteenth century; we can imagine something of the excitement, the confusion, the new alliances which would accompany this process; and of it all, Joshua gives us a summary and simplified account.

## 4. THE STRUGGLE FOR POSSESSION

The invasion then was not a matter of a single swift campaign leaving Israel in tranquil and undisputed possession of the land; and the next two centuries saw a painful struggle for survival in which various groups made their own way, with varying degrees of success but for the most part hemmed in for long periods to the mountainous region in the centre, unable to cope with the Canaanite chariotry in the open country or the strongly fortified cities.

One major disability of the Israelites in this period was their tribal organization, which prevented concerted action against the Canaanite city states. Indeed, the foregoing remarks have made it clear that to speak of "Israel" at all at this time is misleading, since it gives the impression of a unity which was far from being realized. It would be much more correct to speak of "the sons of Israel"—a number of tribes bound together in a confederation. The principle of unity of the confederation was the covenant with God;

its focal point, its centre of attraction, was the Ark of the Covenant, symbol of God's presence amongst them. That is the point of the "covenant-renewal" ceremony described in Joshua 24. We have seen that it is possible that the invaders were able to link up with kinsmen who had not taken part in the Exodus—and had not therefore shared the experience of Sinai. And whether or not that is accepted, it is certainly true that large numbers of the original inhabitants of Canaan joined up with the invaders—we have the actual examples of the family of Rahab (Joshua 6.25) and the people of Gibeon (Joshua 9.3–15). To assimilate all of these to "the sons of Israel" there was only one condition—they must all accept the covenant of Sinai. This covenant, much more than ties of blood, was the principle of unity of the confederation.

This confederation is often called an "amphictyony", on the analogy of the confederation of Greek states (such as the Delphic League) which came together to do battle for some central sanctuary.

This casts great light on the general character of this period. The conquest of Canaan, for example, was looked on as a "holy war"—not quite in the sense of the later *jehad* of Islam, war to spread the faith or to overcome

opposition to it; but in the sense that the battles
in which the tribal league engaged were God's
battles, simply because they were joined in
covenant with him, around his shrine. The
troops drawn up for battle were "the army of
God" and their foes were "the enemies of God".
God is their leader in this warfare; he is consulted before battle, and during it he himself
is engaged in the fighting, using the elements as
his weapons, as when the sun stands still for
Joshua (10.12) or when "the stars in their courses
fought against Sisera" (Judges 5.20). The Ark,
visible sign of God's presence, was the rallying-
point for battle; God was there specifically as
"Yahweh of Hosts", and whenever the Ark was
moved the formula used referred to its role in
battle: "Rise up, Yahweh, and let thine enemies
be scattered", and "'Return, Yahweh, to the hosts
of Israel." (Num. 10.35–6.) The war-cry (*teruah*),
which was originally a savage shout designed to
encourage the combatants and terrify their
enemies, became part of the ritual of the Ark,
and later still took on a purely religious significance in the liturgy of the Temple, as a shout
of acclamation of their God. (Cf. Ps. 95.1,2.) Part
of the routine of preparation for battle was ritual
"sanctification" as for a religious duty (cf.
Joshua 3.5; Deut. 23.10–14); and faith was much
more important than strength of numbers—

Gideon reduces the number of his forces so that the action of God may be more apparent. (Judges 7.1–7.)

Paradoxical as it may appear, it is precisely this character of "holy war" which accounts for much of the brutality associated with this warfare. On several occasions complete extermination of defeated enemies and of their property was said to be ordered. But this was because the victory was God's, not Israel's; and therefore the spoils of victory belonged to God, not them—it was *herem*, anathema, withdrawn from any human usage or claims and set aside for God alone.[8]

The same mentality can also be seen in the quality of the leadership at this time. These leaders were known as *shophetim* (a word which has obvious similarity with the *suffetes*, the title by which the Carthaginian consuls were known). In Hebrew, the root of this word means "to judge"; and it seems probable that it referred to

[8] This total annihilation was obviously not carried out strictly. From a moral point of view, however, what is shocking to a modern reader is the fact that it was even suggested. But this is to demand later standards of morality from a people who were still at a very early stage of their religious development; they were merely acting according to the standards of warfare accepted at that time, and what we should attend to rather is the religious attitude which they imposed on those standards. Cf. again *Witnesses to God*, 62–74.

men who exercised judicial functions in cases of dispute (like Deborah, Judges 4.5). But in the Book of Judges it is used of the military heroes who exercised God's "judgement" on their enemies. The men so described vary considerably. Jephthah was a half-caste outlaw invited to take charge in a time of crisis because of his experience in guerilla warfare. Deborah was a woman of local prestige who stirred up resistance to oppression and called on Barak to lead it. Samson carried on a private vendetta against the Philistines. But one thing they all had in common—that they did not act in virtue of an official position but in virtue of a "charism", endowment by God. For in God's battles who should lead the armies of God but one approved by God? These men, then, were "filled with the Spirit of God" (cf. Judges 3.10:6.34:11.29 etc.) and empowered to perform the great deeds of God.

As might be expected of charismatic leaders, the function of the Judges was essentially temporary and local—they acted in defence of a particular tribe in face of a particular danger. Thus Gideon rallies his own tribe of Manasseh, though Asher, Zebulun and Naphtali join forces with them. The Canticle of Deborah (Judges 5.14–18) lists Ephraim, Machir, Zebulun, Issachar and Naphtali among the combatants, and rebukes Reuben, Gilead, Dan and Asher for failing to answer the call to arms; but it is noticeable that Judah and Simeon are not even mentioned; these southern tribes are apparently so cut off that they were not even expected to join forces with the northern group. This confirms the impression we have seen earlier, of independent tribal activity rather than of concerted national effort.

But since there is no question of the Judges acting as leaders of the whole nation, and since the Book of Judges is clearly a compilation of local traditions about tribal heroes, we cannot merely string these stories together and take it as a history of the whole nation during this period; there were certainly gaps between the various actions; some of them may have overlapped; and we have no guarantee that the order in which they now stand represents the chronological order. In these circumstances, it is not possible to give a complete history of this period.

A good fixed point is probably provided by the victory under Deborah and Barak in the Plain of Esdraelon. This plain, dominated by the Canaanites, formed an impassable barrier which cut off the central tribes from contact with those further north. These tribes formed a coalition, and a providential storm crippled the Canaanite chariotry, which would normally have been decisive in such encounters, and enabled the coalition to win a victory. This was a major breakthrough in the struggle for possession; it gave greater cohesion and therefore greater strength to a large body of the tribes, as well as giving them possession of valuable agricultural land. The date of this battle seems to be about 1125 BC. The Canticle of Deborah puts the site of the battle at "Ta'anak by Megiddo's waters" (Judges 5.19); this suggests that the town of Megiddo, normally much more important than Ta'anak, was not flourishing at this time; and the excavation of Megiddo shows that this was true about 1125 BC.

For the rest, we must be content with seeing in the Book of Judges a good general picture of the period. The picture is one of political chaos. It shows the slow, laborious infiltration of small groups working almost in isolation, cut off from each other partly by their own feeling for independence and partly by the mountainous terrain to which they were limited for much of the time. In their struggle they had to contend not only with the native Canaanites (Deborah and Barak), but with marauding bands from across the Jordan—Edomites[9] and Moabites

---

[9] The Hebrew text speaks of Arameans; but since Othniel is from Debir (Judges 1.13), it seems much more probable that he would have to deal with the nearby

(Othniel and Ehud); and later on, as they became more settled, they were a prey to the raids
of nomadic tribes such as the Midianites (Gideon
is found threshing his corn in secret for fear
of them). In spite of these difficulties, the invaders did manage to adapt themselves fairly
well to the new conditions of life—the story of
Gideon points to their adoption of agriculture,
and other texts mention trading. (Judges 5.17.)

In some ways, they adapted themselves too
well, taking over not only the culture but the
religion of the Canaanites. No doubt the continual references to the worship of "false gods"
in the Book of Judges is partly influenced by the
Deuteronomic editor's religious views; but in the
circumstances something like this was to be
expected, and we do have the evidence of
Gideon, whose other name, Jerubbaal, bears
witness to the influence of pagan religion on even
sincere worshippers of Yahweh; and the story of
Jephthah, who felt it right to sacrifice his
daughter in fulfilment of an oath, shows what
could easily happen when they lived in close
proximity to pagans.

Nevertheless, we might have expected this
process of adaptation to continue and the tribes

Edomites than with the far-off Arameans. The confusion between the words Aram and Edom is very easily
made in Hebrew.

to settle down at least side by side with the Canaanites, if it had not been for a further element in the situation which we have not so far considered and which made a decisive difference. This new factor is the Philistines.

# THE STATE OF ISRAEL

---

## 1. THE PHILISTINE THREAT

THE "People from the Sea", the invaders from the Aegean Islands who attacked Egypt at the end of the thirteenth century (see p. 34), were finally driven off by Ramesses III, and settled on the coast of Canaan. The newcomers included several different groups but they have come down in history under the name of one of them, the Philistines.

They do not seem to have been particularly numerous, but they showed a greater capacity than either the Canaanites or the Israelites for united action. Moreover, they had a tradition of warlike prowess; and above all, they had the monopoly of iron. With these advantages, they began to move inland from their original enclave on the coast, at the same time as the Israelite tribes were making their way westwards. A clash was inevitable. There could, moreover, be hardly any doubt about the outcome of the clash. In Israelite tradition, the Philistines were to become the prototypical "enemy"; they were *the* foreigners, the *alienigenae*; unlike the Canaanites, with whom, after all, the Israelites did have some ties of kinship and some feeling of familiarity, these newcomers were of different race, different tongue, and different customs; they were "the uncircumcized". And the threat they posed was not merely one of warfare, but of extinction. They clearly intended to make themselves complete masters of the land, to make it their own.

The mounting pressure of the Philistines is seen in the migration of the tribe of Dan (Judges 18); and soon the Israelites, who had just succeeded in winning a foothold against Canaanite opposition, found themselves hemmed in once more to the central mountain ridge, with the prospect of worse to come. The story of Samson gives us a good picture of the situation. The scene of Samson's exploits is the Shephelah—the fertile land between the mountains and the sea. Elsewhere, no doubt, other tribes were still struggling for possession of the land, but some of them had advanced so far, and were settling down to agricultural life. But this brought them into close proximity with the Philistine settlement on the coast; and these stories show us what happened. There is no question of a pitched battle; on the contrary, some at least of the Israelites object to Samson troubling their relations with the Philistines, risking reprisals which they would be powerless to resist. But as long as they showed no resistance, relations between the two peoples were peaceful; Samson can even marry a Philistine wife.

But the Israelites could hardly be expected to acquiesce tamely in this subservience. The tone of the stories of Samson suggests that they may have been told to provide some comfort when no more effective resistance was possible. But as the Philistines increasingly asserted their dominion, armed clashes must have become more and more frequent. The decisive clash came about 1050 BC at the battle of Aphek, where the Philistines gained a complete victory—and what was even more disastrous, a victory that involved the capture of the Ark and the burning of Shiloh, the town where it had been stationed.

This was a blow at the very heart of the Covenant People, and one can sense the dismay and despair of the tribes at this shattering of their hopes. The Ark was eventually returned, but its power to rally the tribes for battle was, for the moment at least, lost; and it lay disgraced and ignored in the small village of Kiriath-Jearim. The alliance, however, did survive; the sons of Israel did not succumb entirely to Philistine domination. This was due to the faith and energy of Samuel.

Samuel was a Judge, a charismatic leader who owed his position not to any official appointment, but to the call of God. Probably by temperament, and certainly by force of circumstances, he did not play the part of one of the great heroes of the Holy War to whom the title of Judge had previously been given. He concerned himself with civil functions—settling disputes, as Deborah had done. (Judges 4.4.) But unlike that of Deborah, his activity was not restricted to one place; the text of the Bible shows him "on circuit", so to speak. (1 Sam. 7.16.) And as he went round from place to place, it was not merely petty disputes that he concerned himself with, nor the interpretation of the Covenant law, but with the spirit and faith of the Covenant itself. His activity was largely responsible for holding the tribes together—and indeed for drawing them even closer together, fostering a greater sense of unity which was soon to bear fruit.

Samuel kept alive the spirit of the Covenant People, but he was not the man to lead any great military effort. Guerilla warfare no doubt continued,[1] but this was not sufficient to halt the

[1] 1 Sam. 7.5–12 describes a decisive victory won under Samuel's inspiration; but this hardly fits with the general situation and is best understood as reflecting one aspect or one incident of the resistance led by Samuel. Certainly the concluding words of this passage,

Philistine advance. Eventually the tribes began to look for some more effective means of countering it.

The obvious answer—an answer which Samuel's own activity had surely made more acceptable—was that the total strength of the confederated tribes should be more effectively mobilized. The Philistines were not, after all, such a very formidable enemy—the comparative ease with which they were eventually defeated shows this; but they were certainly more than a match for anything less than the combined forces of all the tribes.

This was obvious; but against this obvious solution there stood certain difficulties, social and historical as well as theological. The Sons of Israel had no strictly national tradition. They were a federation of tribes, and their organization was still only one step removed from the patriarchal system of their semi-nomadic state. And this strong feeling for tribal independence found support in theological theories about "theocracy". From their constitution, from the way in which the federation had come into being, they could have no other ruler than God;

---

"The Philistines were subdued and never again entered Israel's territory", is clearly an anticipation of a much later situation.

and to submit themselves to any permanent form of centralized government could be seen not merely as a distasteful political innovation but as apostasy from the single rule of God.[2]

However, these same theological difficulties also suggested a solution. Because God alone was their ruler, any leader of the Covenant People must be one who acted by divine authority. one in whom the divine spirit manifested itself. Such had been the Judges; and such was the man who now came forward—Saul of Gibeah of the tribe of Benjamin.

## 2. SAUL: AN EXPERIMENT IN MONARCHY

The immediate occasion of his appearance was not directly concerned with the Philistines, but with the Ammonites who attacked and besieged Jabesh-Gilead, in Transjordan; the people of that town appealed to the other tribes for help, and when Saul heard the news, "the spirit of

[2] The biblical account here combines two traditions, one of which sees the monarchy as intended by God (1 Sam. 9.1–10.16), the other anti-monarchic. (1 Sam. 8.1–22:10.17–24.) There is some reason to think that the latter represents later reflection, perhaps even reflection in the light of sad experience of the monarchy, especially in the north. But even if this is so, it is not misleading of the editor to insert it here, since thoughts of this kind must have been in the minds of many at this crisis.

Yahweh burst on him", and in a gesture reminiscent of the heroes of the previous generation he slaughtered the oxen he was driving at the time and sent the pieces round the various tribes, challenging them thus to rally under his leadership to the defence of their brethren.

In the battle which followed he was victorious. And this victory in turn confirmed him as the elect of God in the eyes of the people, and launched him on a series of battles against the enemies of God. Israel was not yet securely established when this major threat from the Philistines threatened them with virtual extinction. During the period of the Judges they had managed to beat off attacks from various quarters, but now many of these enemies took advantage of Israel's difficulties to return to the attack; and Saul had to deal with these. The Bible mentions the Ammonites, Moabites, Edomites, Amalekites and Arameans. (1 Sam. 14.47.)

But obviously Saul's main task was to free the people from the Philistine pressure. In this he was successful; but unfortunately, as so often in the Bible—and as we would expect from this "epic" type of narrative—it is not quite so clear how it was done. It seems to have started with an attack on the Philistine garrison at Michmash, in which Saul's son Jonathan distinguished himself. This gave heart to the rest of the people, who gathered together under Saul's leadership to drive the Philistines out of the mountains.

This was no doubt a wonderful relief for the Israelites, but it was not the end of the war. The Philistines were by no means defeated; this first campaign probably meant little more than a withdrawal of the Philistine outposts in the hill country, while leaving them as before masters of the plain. The Bible points out (1 Sam. 13.19–22) that the Philistine monopoly of iron was so strict that none of the Israelites except Saul and Jonathan possessed as much as a sword. No doubt the flight of the Philistines enabled the Israelites to improve their store of weapons somewhat, but in the plains the Philistine superiority, especially in chariotry, would once more become decisive.

The war dragged on, then; and one of its main casualties was Saul himself. Saul was in many ways an attractive character—simple, generous, impulsive; certainly he won the affection of Samuel himself, even though Samuel eventually found it necessary to break with him. (1 Sam. 15.35.) But there was another side to Saul's character— moody, subject to fits of depression, unsure of himself. It was this side which was brought out by the difficulties of the situation in which he found himself. Saul was a Judge; to call him a "king" is a misleading simplification; the tribes wanted a single leader to organize their full fighting power, a focal point in their covenant war, exactly as the Judges had been— except that the Judges were essentially tribal leaders; even if two, three or even more tribes joined forces under the leadership of a Judge, there was still no question of a "national leader-ship"; whereas in the case of Saul, this was pre-cisely his function, to lead all the tribes together.

From monarchic Judge to king properly so called was a definite step; and Saul's difficulty lay in taking this step—but it was almost equally difficult not to take it. The Judges were charis-matic leaders; but a charism is something which gives power for an occasional function rather than for a permanent one. A man may for a special occasion make such superhuman efforts as give testimony to the spirit within him; but to maintain this as a permanent attitude is quite another matter. But if he does not maintain it, how are the people to believe that he is in fact acting in virtue of the spirit of God? And if he has not that spirit, why should they support him? There is thus a vicious circle: great victories are needed if he is to give proof of his possession of the spirit; but he cannot gain great victories without popular support—which will not be forthcoming unless he gives proof of possessing the spirit. He needs popular support for success, but he cannot succeed without popular support.

There was moreover no precedent for his position. Such precedent as there was worked against him. Gideon, for example, after having delivered the people as Judge, was offered kingship, and refused it precisely on the grounds that such a position was contrary to the constitution of a theocracy. True, there was Abimelech; but his experiment in royalty was short-lived and discredited from the beginning by its association with the Canaanites. Saul's position was certainly an innovation, and it would have taken a stronger character than Saul to find his way safely through the problems which it raised to an acceptable solution. Even from the beginning there were scornful voices raised about his suitability for the position; these voices were silenced by the clear manifestation of the spirit of God in his first battle, but they would always be there, ready to be raised as soon as there was any setback.

All this difficulty and uncertainty imposed a continual strain on Saul. We have a clear indication of the anxiety which must always have been at the back of his mind in the incident related in 1 Sam. 13.6–15; in the face of a Philistine attack, his forces were melting away—precisely the thing he was always terrified of. To halt the

stream of desertion he felt that he had somehow
to bring into play the religious ideals which lay
closest to the hearts of the people, to recall them
to the spirit of the holy war. So he took it upon
himself to offer the sacrifice which preceded
battle. Besides betraying the anxiety which
weighed on him, this illustrates another aspect
of his difficult position—the conflict between
civil and religious authority which the position
of a king involved. Israel's constitution was such
that the distinction between religious and
secular—never very clear-cut in any ancient
society—was particularly difficult to decide. God
alone was their ruler, and his authority covered
all aspects of life, civil as well as religious. But
this did not automatically mean that the king
was God's delegate in both spheres. This in fact
was precisely the question at issue—what sort of
office the kingship was, what exactly was the
authority which God intended him to have;
was it simply leadership in battle, or did it
include religious functions as well? There was,
after all, a priestly class—of which Samuel was
the representative—to whom such functions belonged by right. It was not merely a question of
this isolated action of offering sacrifice; this
Abraham had done before him, and David was
to do after him; but what caused Samuel to object was not professional jealousy but the feeling

that Saul was here going beyond his calling.
He was called to be the leader in war, and he
was here claiming religious functions as well; he
was making religion an instrument in his task,
instead of submitting himself humbly as an
instrument of the divine will.

The breach with Samuel was probably the last
straw for Saul; henceforth he was beset by something very like a persecution mania; he began
to see treachery on every side, even among his
army, even in his own family. And while he was
squandering time and energy pursuing these
shadows, the Philistines gathered their strength
again for another attack. They had by now
realized that only in the plains could they count
on a definite superiority; so their forces massed
in the Plain of Jezrael, hoping to tempt Saul's
forces down from the mountains.[3] Astonishingly,
the Israelites did in fact accept the challenge—
perhaps they thought that even in the plain they
would be more than a match for the enemy so

[3] A preliminary notice to the battle in 1 Sam. 29.1
says that the Philistines first massed at Aphek, and that
it was Saul who chose Jezrael as the site for battle. But it
is difficult to understand why the Philistines would
gather at Aphek when Saul's forces were so far away;
nor can one imagine both sides mustering at Aphek
and then involving themselves in the long march north
to Jezrael, where the battle certainly took place. It is
possible that this reference to Aphek is a reminiscence
of the first great Philistine victory there, 1 Sam. 4.12.

far from his base; or perhaps by now Saul (the Bible here inserts the story of his visit to the Witch of Endor) was so far gone in despair that he cast prudence to the winds. The result was an overwhelming victory for the Philistines. The Israelites tried to flee back to the hills, but the Philistines pursued and inflicted great slaughter on the disorganized rabble. And it was here, on Mount Gilboa, that Saul was cornered and fell by his own hand—a fittingly tragic end to a tragic life.

### 3. David and the Establishment of Monarchy

One of the victims of Saul's jealousy was a young man of the Tribe of Judah, called David. He had distinguished himself fighting against the Philistines[4]; and to the king's frame of mind in those days, his success and popularity made him an inevitable object of suspicion—a suspicion which went as far as attempted murder. David then took to the hills of Judah and lived as an outlaw with a small band of kinsmen and

---

[4] Here again the Bible incorporates two traditions. According to one, David first appeared in public life as a sort of squire attached to Saul; according to the other he is an unknown shepherd visiting his brothers in the army, and first comes to Saul's notice by his defeat of Goliath.

supporters. But even here Saul pursued him,
and eventually he fled outside Israelite territory,
to the Philistines.

He offered his services to the Philistine city of
Gath, and the ruler of this city, Achis, gladly
accepted him. The understanding was that David
would receive the revenues from the town of
Ziklag, not far from the Israelite town of Beer-
sheba, in return for assisting the Philistines by
armed raids against his old enemy, Saul. But
David had no intention of changing sides; he
solved this dilemma by assisting the Philistines
indeed, but by carrying out raids on the desert
tribes who were a menace both to the Philistines
and to Israel.

David spent more than a year in this way, and
during that period his following increased.
Thus, when the news of Saul's death arrived he
was able to return home at the head of a ready-
made army of seasoned troops and was accepted
by his own people of Judah as their natural
leader.

In the north, however, a few of Saul's loyal
supporters, headed by his commander-in-chief,
Abner, had regrouped on the far side of the
Jordan, well out of reach of the victorious Philistines; and there they presented Saul's son Ishbaal as his rightful successor. This was a
dangerous situation; it threatened a rivalry

between north and south which seems to correspond to some deeper division between the tribes (we have already noted how, for example, the Canticle of Deborah takes no account whatever of the southern tribes). Very wisely, David refrained from direct action. Ishbaal roused no great enthusiasm among the northern tribes, and David saw that there was every chance that in time they would come over to his side of their own accord. To use force would only antagonize them, so he even tried to restrain his own troops in the raids by which Abner sought to provoke him to battle.

His hopes were fulfilled. Ishbaal eventually alienated Abner, who was really his sole support; and shortly after this he was assassinated. There was now no alternative to David as ruler of all Israel.

One of David's first actions[5], and certainly one of the most important in its implications and consequences, was the choice of a new capital. The place chosen for this purpose was the ancient Canaanite stronghold of Jerusalem. Its

[5] This is the order given by the Bible. It may be thought more probable that David would have to drive off the Philistines first before setting up his capital in the heart of country at that time under their control. But this is not conclusive, as the text shows—the Philistines may well have regarded David tolerantly as one of their allies.

4

favourable position—on a hill difficult of access on three sides and easily defended to the north —which made it attractive to David, made it equally difficult to capture. It had resisted Israelite attacks so far, and the inhabitants were confident that it could resist David also. But David's troops succeeded, apparently by making their way up the tunnel which led from the spring of Gihon to the interior of the city. David then took up residence there and made it the centre of government.

The significance of this move went far beyond merely the establishment of a new capital. In the first place, it was not a new capital, but the first Israel had ever had. It was a decisive step towards the unification of the nation. This had been initiated under Saul, but after Saul's death a dangerous split developed between the northern and the southern tribes. This new capital, newly captured, was free from any traditional associations which would prejudice it in the eyes of either north or south. Even geographically it was more central than either Hebron, from where David had ruled Judah, or Shiloh, the old cultic centre where the Ark had been stationed.

It was a token also of a wider unity, the unity of the state. In spite of Israel's determined efforts and ruthless ambition, not all the

Canaanite cities had been overcome; up and
down the land there were many pockets of
Canaanite resistance which the Israelite invasion
had left untouched. From the time of David
onwards there is no further mention of these, so
it is to be presumed that they were absorbed into
the new state; some of them by conquest, like
Jerusalem itself, but many others by freely
throwing in their lot with the new state which
was so clearly emerging. It is significant that
there is no mention of David annihilating the
population of Jerusalem after he captured it,
as there is in other instances of Israelite victory;
admittedly, in these other cases, too, it is sometimes the expression of a theological principle,
the ideal of the holy war (cf. p. 69 and note),
rather than of a historical fact; but nevertheless
the capture of Jerusalem does stand as the symbol of a new stage of events, one in which there
is a state composed of various nationalities all
recognizing the authority of one central government.[6]

Unity of the nation, unity of the state; but the
most important significance attached to Jerusalem was the unity of Church and State. When

[6] Perhaps there is a reference to this in Ps. 110.4;
David is presented as priest-king, legitimate successor
of Melchizedek, the ancient Canaanite priest-king of
Jerusalem.

we reflect on David's career, shorn of the idealization of later tradition, we may well have the picture of a military dictator, a despot who seized
power by a combination of armed force and
skilful opportunism: a benevolent despot indeed,
and one whose rule was for the most part welcomed and who exercised his power wisely; but
how far removed from Saul, king by popular
acclaim, how far from the simple tribal confederacy which marched out of the desert! Yet
this tribal confederacy lay at the very heart of
the people which David ruled, in the sense that
the Covenant which bound them to their God
was the very principle of their existence. And
now—this is what saves David from the charge
of despotic ambition—David shows himself
clearly aware of this; and by a simple stroke of
genius he links Israel's most sacred traditions
with the new regime. The Ark, symbol of God's
presence with Israel as God of the Covenant,
and ancient rallying-point of the tribes, was last
heard of in a little village near the borders of
Philistine territory. Now David has it resurrected
from its obscurity and has it transferred with
great pomp and ceremony to his new city. So he
makes it plain that he is not imposing despotic
rule at whatever cost to the ideals of his subjects; he is not making a complete break with the
past; on the contrary, the past continues safely

in his hands; his capital is the covenant shrine, and the subjects of the monarchy are still the Covenant People.

In contemporary civilizations the king was looked on as a sacred person. Israel, because of the belief in a personal and transcendent God, could not go so far as other countries—as Egypt, for example, where the kings were thought to be merely successive embodiments of the god. But this attitude did lend itself easily to combination with the covenant idea, by which God and the nation were inseparably linked. The king was the representative of the nation; and the covenant with the nation was now focused on the king in particular.[7] Assyrian kings were said to be the adopted sons of God; so was Israel's king (Ps. 2.7)—but in this he was also representing the nation as a whole, which was God's son. (Exod. 4.22.) The function of the king in other societies of the time—the function of government in any society—was the welfare of the state: protection against enemies from without, justice within, and the prosperity which results from this peace. In contemporary thought this was represented magically, as if the king's own strength ensured the fertility of the land; the king even impersonated the god in the myth of

[7] This is expressed in the form of an oracle to David in 2 Sam. 7.4–16.

the dying and rising god, which re-enacted the
cycle of nature and thus ensured renewal of the
annual miracle of spring growth. But in Israel,
this peace and prosperity were the object of the
Covenant hopes, so that again it was here easy
to combine contemporary ideas with their own
traditions by transferring the fulfilment of these
hopes to the king. Psalm 72 expresses this
clearly:

> God, give thy judgement to the king,
> Thy justice to the son of the king,
> That he may judge thy people rightly
> And give judgement for the poor.
> Mountains and hills bring forth peace . . .
> He will come down like rain on the grass,
> Like dew that moistens the earth . . .
> The kings of Seba and Sheba will bring him
>     gifts,
> All kings will bow down before him . . .

The psalm stresses the "justice" required of a
king, especially justice for the poor and helpless
(those who have no other hope of redress, those
who cannot win their case by bribery, see p. 170).
For the king in Israel is not a despot; he is not
himself a god nor does he take the place of God.
He is subject to God's law and the custodian of
it; at his enthronement, God's "decree" is
handed to him, and this decree is both the divine

oracle (cf. Ps. 2.7, referring to 2 Sam. 7), the patent of his royalty, and the royal charter enunciating his rights and duties.[8]

The king, therefore, embodies the Covenant; in token of his sacred character he is anointed, and this gives rise to the royal title *Messiah*, a title which becomes a summary of Israel's covenant ideal.

## 4. THE FOUNDATION OF EMPIRE

David's immediate task, however, was to deal with the Philistine menace. The defeat of Saul had left the Philistines more firmly entrenched than ever in the central mountains. They looked indulgently on David's accession to power in the south—no doubt they still regarded him as one of their vassal kings. But the union of the whole nation under him roused their suspicions, and they decided to take action. But their action was hampered by the mountainous terrain which cancelled out their superiority in armament; whereas David had played hide-and-seek with Saul's men for years in these very mountains and it was terrain which suited him ideally. By guerilla tactics he wore down the Philistine

[8] Cf. 1 Sam. 10.25, "Samuel expounded the royal protocol to the people and put it in writing"; and Ps. 101 no doubt gives us an example of the king's responsibilities.

attack, and gradually forced them to withdraw from the mountains. But the decisive move was his decision not to stop there—this had been Saul's error, allowing the Philistines time to regroup and renew the attack. As usual, the Bible is lacking in details, but it makes it clear that David followed up his victory over the Philistines in the mountains by pursuing them on their home ground, back even as far as the Philistine town of Gezer. It is a measure of the extent of his success that the Philistines never again troubled the peace of Israel, and indeed the next time we hear of them it is as bodyguards in David's army. (2 Sam. 8.18.)

David was then able to turn his attention to relations with other countries near by. With the Ammonites in Transjordan he tried to establish peaceful relationships, and sent ambassadors for that purpose. But the Ammonites were suspicious of this move and insulted the ambassadors. David was enraged by this gratuitous insult, and ordered general mobilization. The Ammonites called on various Aramean tribes for support; but Joab, in charge of the Israelite army, divided his forces into two groups, and leaving one to contain the Ammonites, led the others against the Arameans and drove them off. This left him free to deal with the Ammonites. The only organized resistance he met was in the capital, Rabbah, but he encircled the town and eventually broke in. He then sent for David (who meanwhile had been engaged in the shameful episode with Bathsheba, the wife of one of his soldiers) so that the king should have the honour of the final victory. David then claimed royal power over the country, and the population was subjected to forced labour.

David then turned his attention to the Arameans who had lent their support against him in the recent campaign. These states[9] to the north of Israel were an obvious potential source of trouble, especially since one of them, the kingdom of Zobah, had gained control of several others and was trying to extend its power still further. The King of Zobah, Hadadezer, formed a strong coalition, which included also the kingdom of Damascus, to meet the Israelite attack; but David defeated them and took large quantities of booty. This was further increased by a gift from the King of Hamath, in gratitude for this defeat of an uncomfortably powerful neighbour. David then appointed his own nominees as governors of these states and imposed tribute on them.

Edom and Moab too—on what pretext we do

[9] It has been thought more convenient to hold over a fuller account of the Arameans till p. 143, in a context where their influence is more important.

not know—were ruthlessly subdued and made vassals of Israel.

Thus, within the space of some thirty years David raised Israel from the position of a confederation of tribes struggling for existence to a leading position in the world of that time. Israel itself was a unified state—covenant tribes, Canaanite city states, and presumably Philistines too. Beyond their borders there were subject states of various degrees—Edom and Moab vassal states under their own rulers, Ammon at least nominally under David's direct rule as king, and the Arameans under governors appointed by the Israelite king.

Internally, the main development was in the organization of the army. David still made use of the theory surviving from their nomadic state that the whole nation was a people in arms—each tribe was supposed to contribute a certain number of men to the national army in times of battle. (Cf. 2 Sam. 10.7.) But in addition to this popular army, Saul already had begun the custom of attaching men permanently to his service (1 Sam. 14.52); and David continued the process—we have already seen the importance of this band of trained men, gathered round him when he was outlawed, in his rise to power. This standing army of professional soldiers, maintained by the booty of their victories, included

foreign mercenaries, men like Uriah the Hittite. Among these in turn are singled out an
elite, the "heroes" listed in 2 Sam. 23.8ff; and
what would appear to be the king's personal
bodyguard, the Pheletians and Keretians (Philistines and Cretans).

Apart from this David appears to have made
no great change in the internal organization of
the country. The normal running of the country
was left in the hands of the traditional tribal
authorities, with the king acting as a final court
of appeal. (Cf. 2 Sam. 15.2.)

## 5. The Struggle for Succession

Through the skill and prudence of David, the
constitutional question of the monarchy which
Saul had failed to solve was now settled. It was
even settled that David's descendants were to be
his successors in the monarchy. But this did not
automatically establish the principle that it was
the eldest son who was to succeed; and this uncertainty gave rise to intrigues within the royal
family.

The first attempt came from David's son
Absalom. He assassinated his elder brother
Amnon because of an outrage he had committed
against Absalom's sister. Because of this he was
sent into exile, and took refuge with his mother's

family in the Aramean town of Geshur (she was
the daughter of the King of Geshur); but three
years later he was allowed to return, and immediately set about winning himself popularity
and influence among the people. When he
thought his plans were sufficiently advanced he
moved to Hebron, the old capital of Judah, and
made arrangements for the final step; he let it be
known that he was going to be proclaimed king
there, and hoped that this would be followed
by such overwhelming popular acclaim that
David would be forced to recognize it and give
way. His plans seem to have proceeded with surprising secrecy, for it was only at this last
moment that the court heard of it, and the news
was followed by alarm and confusion. David
realized that Absalom's first objective must be
the capital, so he promptly left the city and re-
treated across the Jordan and northwards to
Mahanaim. Absalom meanwhile entered Jerusalem, but instead of following up his advantage
at once he delayed there to consolidate his position. This lost him the initiative which surprise
had given him; it gave David time to take stock
of the position and see the full extent of the
danger; and this was at once seen to be much less
serious than was at first thought. It became clear
that it was not a mass popular uprising, but one
which had been artificially provoked and had

relatively few wholehearted supporters. In the
course of his flight David had received evidence
of continuing loyalty to him, and even in Jerusalem there were supporters who kept him informed of Absalom's plans. Most of all, the army
remained true to him, and this was decisive.
When eventually Absalom's forces moved to the
attack, David's trained and experienced profes-
sionals inflicted a crushing defeat on them which
put an end to the rebellion. Absalom, against
David's orders, was put to death.

This ended this particular danger; but it did
not settle the real difficulty, which was the doubt
about the succession. And as David grew old, the
trouble broke out again, this time from
Absalom's younger brother, Adonijah. This
time, moreover, it was rather more serious.
Absalom's revolt had been a matter of personal
ambition, and never had any influential backing. At one time Absalom thought he could
count on the support of Joab, David's commander-in-chief; it was Joab's intervention
which had caused the sentence of banishment to
be rescinded; but after Absalom's return, Joab
made it clear that this was as far as he was prepared to go, and finally it was his hand that
hurled the spear which ended the revolt and
Absalom's life. But now, when Adonijah made
it clear that he considered himself David's

natural successor, Joab did lend him his support; so did the priest Abiathar. No doubt there were personal rivalries involved, for Benaiah, the commander of the guard, and Zadok, the other priest of the Jerusalem shrine, lent their support to another son of David, Solomon. But at least it is clear that the most influential members of David's court thought it was time that this issue was settled.

This time, however, they did not allow it to reach the stage of rebellion. While Adonijah was carrying on discussions with his supporters, Solomon's party approached the king himself and urged him to take action. The king agreed. Quickly but with all due ceremony, Solomon was installed as king. The proclamation of this was enough to put an end to Adonijah's plans, and his support melted away. David then resigned authority into the hands of Solomon, and the transition was safely accomplished.

## 6. Solomon: "Happy and Glorious"

The Bible devotes quite ample space to the account of Solomon's reign; but on reading it we discover surprisingly few facts. It is not so much a history of his reign as a picture of a monarch "happy and glorious"—and for this facts are less important than epithets. But this is not to say that it is a completely idealized picture, and from it we can gain a fair impression of the period.

Solomon's first care was to consolidate the authority so hastily conferred on him. Adonijah's life was spared, but on surety of his good behaviour; and it took just one slip for this surety to be demanded. Adonijah sought permission to take as his wife one of David's harem; this was taken as an indication that he had not given up all hope of inheriting David's kingdom also—perhaps rightly, but no doubt Solomon was glad enough of the opportunity, and Adonijah paid the forfeit for his rashness with his life. Abiathar, the priest, escaped most lightly; he was merely dismissed to the small town of Anathoth. Joab, seeing the way things were going, took refuge in the shrine of the Ark; but this did not deter his rival Benaiah, who killed him there by the altar.

Thus all the leading figures of the rival party were eliminated, and Solomon had no further opposition to his authority until the end of his life.

The same is true of his authority in the kingdom as a whole; not for him the almost incessant wars and struggles which had marked David's reign. David had done his work well, and Solomon merely entered into his inheritance. This is not to say that his reign was one of idyllic serenity undisturbed by the clamour of war. We hear of trouble in two of the states which David had subdued. In Edom, only one member of the ruling family had escaped the massacre which followed Joab's victory there; he had taken refuge in Egypt, and now that David and Joab were dead he returned to claim his throne and refused to recognize Israel's supremacy. And in the north, similarly, the leader of one of the Aramean bands which David had managed to bring under his control now seized power in Damascus and claimed independence from Israel.

Moreover, Solomon maintained a standing army far greater than that of David. The most striking innovation in this army was the powerful chariot force, numbering, we are told, 1400 chariots. This is a significant contrast to David's policy; when David defeated the Arameans, a large force of chariots and horses fell into his hands, but he could think of nothing better to do with them than to hamstring the horses. (2 Sam. 8.4.) But now Solomon had both the skilled troops to man the chariots and the financial resources to maintain them. The chariotry was stationed at a series of garrison towns stretching from Hazor in the north to Tamar in the south, strategically placed so as to command the approaches to the centre of the country, and near an open plain where chariots could be used to advantage. At least some of these towns were ancient Canaanite strongholds, but Solomon strengthened the fortifications and improved the facilities; excavations at Megiddo have brought to light the magnificent covered stables there, sufficient for 430 horses.

Nevertheless, it is true to say that Solomon was not a warrior king. We do not even know what steps he took against the rebellions of Edom and Damascus[10]; and in general, the security and prosperity of the State were assured in his day by peaceful means—diplomacy was as characteristic of his reign as conquest had been of David's.

We can see some trace of his diplomatic policy in the marriages he contracted—taking it that at least many of these would be connected with political alliances. The mention of "seven hundred wives of royal rank and three hundred concubines" may legitimately be suspected of exaggeration; a king's harem being a sign of

[10] According to 2 Chron. 8.4, Solomon captured Hamath-zobah and Tadmor (Palmyra); one may be slightly hesitant about this because of the Chronicler's systematic tendency to glorify the monarchy—the verse immediately preceding this passage gives us an example, attributing to Solomon a gift of cities *from* Hiram which the equivalent passage in Kings (1 Kings 9.11) tells us was a gift *to* Hiram. But on the other hand, Solomon's plans for commercial expansion would demand that he should secure his trade routes to the north.

wealth and power, this would merely be an admissible way of expressing his glory. But the text also mentions explicitly Edomite, Moabite, Ammonite and Hittite princesses; and no doubt these represent treaties by which Solomon maintained and extended what his father had won. The same deduction may be drawn from his marriage to an Egyptian princess, and in this case it is even more significant; for it is the senior partner in an alliance who receives a princess for his harem—along with the rich dowry which, as in this case, she brings with her. When the great Egyptian king, Amenophis III, made a treaty with the Mitanni (p. 28), it was the latter who gave up his daughter to seal the alliance; but now it is the Egyptian princess who comes to the court of Israel, thus showing the pre-eminence to which the state had risen.

The marriage with a Sidonian princess indicates an alliance which was to have a particular influence on Solomon's course. This Phoenician state, with its seat of government at Tyre, represents practically the last remnants of Canaanite independence after the incursions of Israel and the Peoples of the Sea in the south and the Arameans in the north.[11] At this time it

[11] On the Phoenicians, see W. F. Albright, "The Role of the Canaanites in the History of Civilization", in *The Bible and the Ancient Near East*, ed. G. Ernest Wright (1961), 341–8.

was embarked on a period of commercial expansion by means of sea-trade; and by this treaty, impetus was given to Solomon's own trading activities.

The Israelites were never great sailors, but with Phoenician help Solomon constructed a merchant fleet and manned it with Phoenicians to train his own men. There was no satisfactory port on the Mediterranean coast—and besides, the Mediterranean trade was already in the hands of his northern ally; so the fleet was based on Ezion-Geber, at the head of the Gulf of Aqaba, and from there undertook trading voyages round the Arabian peninsula, bringing back gold, silver, ivory, spices—as well as apes and peacocks!

These goods were purchased by exports from the metal works at Ezion-Geber. These are not mentioned in the Bible, but the mines and smelting works found in that district are dated to Solomon's time. This development too is probably due to Phoenician influence; they exploited the metal industry so thoroughly that the word for a foundry, "tarshish", was given to their settlements in Cyprus, Sardinia and Spain[12]; and the great ships built to carry on this trade were known as "ships of Tarshish".

The state visit of the Queen of Sheba was connected with these activities of Solomon; in

[12] Cf. Albright, 341, 347.

spite of the royal pomp with which it was surrounded, it would not be too much to see it as a
trade delegation, with the small Arabian state
putting on show the goods it had to offer—gold,
precious stones, perfumes and spices. It seems
hardly likely that all of this would be for internal
consumption, and most of it was doubtless re-
exported to other countries. For Israel was now
in a position to take advantage of its fortunate
geographical situation and control a large part
of the caravan trade. This certainly appears to
have been the case with the trade in chariots
mentioned in 1 Kings 10.28f; horses were im-
ported from Cilicia and chariots from Egypt, and
then resold. With all this wealth flowing into the
country, one can well understand the feeling of
the people of the time, that "silver was as common as stone and cedars as common as syca-
mores." (1 Kings 10.27.)

### 7. LITERARY ACTIVITY

With this great surge forward of the economy
went an increase in literary activity. The art of
writing had long been known, but Israel had
neither felt the need to use it extensively nor
had the opportunity to do so in her struggling
history so far. But the Canaanites and Egyptians
were already proficient in the art; and when the

growing needs of his administration demanded the use of writing it was to these countries that Solomon looked for models, and perhaps also for scribes. (See p. 55.) The excavation of other ancient archives, such as those of Mari, Tell el-Amarna or Ugarit, gives us some idea of what this would entail. There would be first of all records of financial transactions—accounts, taxes, receipts. Then there would be political records—dealings with other rulers such as Hiram of Tyre would be carried on at least partly by correspondence; and there would be records of treaties and agreements with these states. There would be administrative lists—lists of officials, lists of administrative districts.

A natural development from this would be some form of annals; and from this in turn something like a genuine history would evolve. The annals of the kings of Judah and of Israel are mentioned explicitly in the Bible (e.g., 1 Kings 14.19,29). 1 Kings 11.41 refers to a "History of Solomon" which seems to have formed the basis of the Bible's account of his reign. Above all there is the splendid "History of the Succession" which runs from 2 Sam. 9 to 20 and is continued in 1 Kings 1–2.

Then there were the traditions of earlier days which had been handed down by word of mouth; no doubt these, too, now began to take shape in writing; the account of the invasion of Canaan, for example, or the great deeds of various local heroes, which form the basis of the present books of Joshua and Judges.

Another type of literature which is characteristic of this era, and indeed associated particularly with Solomon himself, is known as the Wisdom literature. What wisdom meant for Israel can be seen from the account given of Solomon's wisdom: "Solomon's wisdom surpassed the wisdom of all the people of the east, and all the wisdom of Egypt . . . he spoke of the trees, from the cedar that is in Lebanon to the hyssop that grows out of the wall; he spoke also of beasts and of birds and of fish." (1 Kings 4.30–33.) It is concerned with factual information about the practical sciences. It deals also with the equally pragmatic insight into human nature which is essential for one in authority, as the Bible shows by its example of Solomon's judgement in the case of two women disputing over a child. (1 Kings 3.16–28.) But it deals especially with practical instruction to young men on how to conduct themselves in society, and then in a wider sense with right conduct in general. This instruction was given in gnomic, proverbial sayings, examples of which (some of them attributed to Solomon himself) are to be found in the Book of Proverbs.

The liturgical development which also took place in Israel at this time would also call for appropriate literature, especially hymns to be used at the various ceremonies. These hymns, the Psalms, were naturally influenced by Canaanite models, and some of them may even be due to Canaanite musicians.[13]

But undoubtedly the greatest work of this period—and great by any standards—is the work which is conventionally denoted by the symbol "J". This modest anonymity is not altogether to be regretted, since its directs our attention not to the activity of an individual author but to the whole body of tradition which his work embodies. In Israel, as in any other nation with a certain history behind it, an immense amount of oral literature was in circulation, of many different forms, dealing with many different subjects. Some of it consisted of snatches of verse (like the "Song of the Wells", Num. 21.17–18), some of it consisted of prose narratives.

[13] Cf. *The Old Testament and Modern Study*, ed. H. H. Rowley, 188. According to 1 Chron. 25.1, the sons of Asaph, of Heman and of Jeduthun (or Ethan) were responsible for the music in the liturgy, and these names are found in the titles to several of the Psalms— e.g., 73–83, 89 etc. In 1 Kings 4.31 Heman and Ethan are called "wise men", skilled in music. The names are not Israelite, and the text calls Ethan an "Ezrahite", i.e., probably "a native", a Canaanite.

Some of it was directly religious in character, some of it dealt with ordinary secular events. There were fragments of folklore, stories about ancestors, stories of family feuds. There were even stories from the very remote past which belonged to the common stock of tradition of many nations of the ancient Near East. Some of them were traditions peculiar to certain tribes, some were told in connection with certain places —especially "holy places" which thus justified their reputation. And above all there was the great *geste* of the Exodus which, in accordance with the ancient rubric which bade the Israelites hand on the story to their descendants (Exod. 12.26ff, Deut. 6.20–5), was recounted annually at the great feasts in the central sanctuary.

But by this time Israel was no longer a collection of tribes; it was a nation. And it was no longer fully occupied with the struggle for existence; its existence was assured and it had reached that stage of self-consciousness in which the need was felt to express its self-awareness; to look back over the past and in the light of that past to declare its identity and national character. What was the national character? Israel's conviction was that they were a unique people with a unique relationship to the only God. And now this anonymous genius, J, found the means to give expression to that faith in an epic which puts the history of the nation into the context of the whole of created time. Surveying the scattered collection of tribal traditions, this author selected, arranged and organized the material so as to present a single account which runs from the creation right down to the Exodus, and which at the same time gave expression to the deepest truths about the position of man with God, and the position of Israel at the heart of the whole.[14]

## 8. BUILDING ACTIVITY

Israel's new prosperity is also to be seen in the building activities of this period. The process of sedentarization was by now more or less complete; but sedentarization is not synonymous with "urbanization". As in Canaan, not all the citizens of a town lived within its walls; they carried on their lives in the countryside around the town (which was usually quite small by modern standards, no more than a village), and looked to it for their market and for protection.

[14] This account of J's work represents the common view of most scholars today. For discussion of disputed points, as well as for more detailed analysis of J, reference may be made to works dealing with the literature of the Pentateuch: e.g., A. Weiser, *Introduction to the Old Testament* (1961), 74–110; or Robert and Feuillet, *Introduction à la Bible*, vol. 1, 331–42, 348–61.

There was a great increase in the number of these towns in this period, due partly to the invention of waterproof lime plaster, which enabled water to be caught in cisterns, and thus made it possible for people to form a settlement wherever there was rain, instead of, as previously, only where there was a river or a well or an oasis.

Both in the fortification of the towns and in the buildings within them, the Israelites were usually content to take over the Canaanite constructions; indeed there was a general deterioration in standards—there were no sewers and no streets; houses were roughly huddled together in groups which probably corresponded to clan groupings. This is to be expected of a people just beginning to adopt a sedentary life, and in the course of the monarchy a gradual improvement is to be seen.[15]

This improvement takes effect first in royal buildings. We have already referred to the garrison towns which Solomon rebuilt, and to the stables of Megiddo. But naturally it was Jerusalem, the king's own city and the seat of government, which received most attention. The

[15] For further details on the buildings of this period, see W. F. Albright, *The Archaeology of Palestine* (1949), 113–27; F. du Buit, *Biblical Archaeology*, Faith and Fact Books (1960), 21–5.

original Jebusite town, the "City of David", was quite small, occupying the hill between the Kidron valley on the east and the Tyropean on the west.[16] But as the number of inhabitants increased it began to spread westwards beyond the Tyropean valley; and to the north Solomon constructed a complex of buildings which would make Jerusalem a capital worthy of the nation.

David had already a palace in the city, but the remarkable growth of the state made this now inadequate. So between the City of David and the hill north of it the ground was filled in and levelled off[17] and made the site of a group of administrative buildings. The nucleus of this group was the palace—the king's own apartments and a separate establishment for the queen, built in the first place for Pharao's daughter. The first of the public rooms of the palace was the throne-room, in which stood Solomon's magnificent throne of gold and ivory with arm-rests carved in the shape of standing lions, and crouching lions on either side of the six steps which led up to the throne. Here most of the public business of the kingdom was carried

[16] The modern Jerusalem—the walls of which were built in the sixteenth century by Suleiman the Magnificent—is much closer to the site of the Roman Aelia Capitolina than to that of ancient Jerusalem. This lay in general further south than the modern city.

[17] This is the Millo referred to in 1 Kings 9.15.

on, in particular the administration of justice. At the entrance to the palace stood the guard-room, where the king's bodyguard was stationed; 1 Kings 10.16–17, describes the golden shields which hung there, and no doubt the guard would make a fine show on ceremonial occasions, but they had arms of more practical use also. (Cf. Isa. 22.8.) This guard-room was called the "House of the Forest of Lebanon" because of the pillars of cedar wood which were a notable feature of its construction.

This is all that the text mentions on this subject. It is true that the whole work of central government revolved round the king, so that the palace lay at the heart of the government; but besides the luxurious household which we know Solomon maintained, there was an increasingly complex system of government offices, and all of this could not be contained in merely a large mansion. We may presume, then, that at least in time a much larger group of administrative buildings would be added, which the text neglects to mention.

But undoubtedly the masterpiece of Solomon's buildings, the crowning glory of the city and the nation, was the Temple. Many details of the architecture of the Temple are vague[18]; but since

[18] On the Temple, see De Vaux, *Ancient Israel* (1961), 312–21, and A. Parrot, *The Temple of Jerusalem*

it was built with Canaanite help, no doubt it would follow the model of Canaanite temples. It was a long rectangular building of dressed stone, panelled with cedar and cypress wood. In front of the building stood two massive pillars, the equivalent of the Canaanite *masseboth* referred to frequently in the Bible (e.g. Gen. 28.18; Isa. 19.19); these were memorial pillars, commemorating the appearance of the divinity and ultimately coming to represent the god in person. In the Temple this idolatrous connotation could hardly be accepted; they were here partly traditional *motifs* and partly symbolic.

The plan of the building corresponded to Canaanite ideas of the holiness of God, which Israel shared. Just as God was holy, that is to say, "cut off" from the human world, so anything associated with him was cut off from profane use. Any holy place, any place associated with God, was surrounded by an area of holiness—so the whole of Mount Sinai when God appeared there; the Israelites were told not to set foot on it, lest they should die. In the same way, then, the whole Temple area was composed of increasing degrees of holiness. There was first of

(1957). Both of these give fuller discussion of the problems connected with the building as well as a fuller account of the details and furnishings than is necessary here.

all the courtyard in which the Temple stood; then the building itself had first of all a porch, then the body of the building which was more sacred still, and finally within this the small chamber which was "the Holy of Holies".

In pagan temples, this small inner sanctuary contained an idol of the god. In the Temple of Jerusalem, there was the Ark of the Covenant. This Ark was a box which contained a copy of the Covenant laws, but it symbolized the presence of God himself. When it was brought into the Temple a cloud was said to have filled the building (1 Kings 8.6–11); and this cloud expresses the transcendence of God, his majesty, which is beyond human sight; and the darkness of the room in which it was placed suggests the same idea. (Cf. Isa. 6.1–3.) The Ark itself was looked on as God's throne, or sometimes he was thought of as invisibly enthroned above the Ark, so that the Ark itself was his footstool. On either side of the Ark were statues known as "cherubs"; these correspond to the Babylonian *karibu*, the winged beings which were guardians of the temples; and no doubt these could be imagined as playing the same part in relation to Yahweh's throne as the lions did in relation to Solomon's throne described above.

The building of the Temple did not mark the beginning of formal religious worship in Israel.

This began with the Covenant itself, with their sojourn at Mount Sinai. But the religious ideas formulated there were a basis for development; and we may now try to take stock of this development, to see the connection between the religion of Sinai and the religion of the monarchic state.

## 9. DEVELOPMENT IN RELIGION

Every department of life in Israel had a religious aspect. This was indeed true of all people of the time, but it was particularly true of Israel because of their character as a covenant people—a people whose very existence was intimately bound up with God. Besides the ancient custom of dedicating the seventh day to God, and the monthly observance of the new moon,[19] there were ceremonies attached to every great moment of life—purification and consecration in connection with death, marriage and childbirth. Much of this ceremonial was derived from a quite primitive stage of religion; there is something akin to the idea of taboo in the distinction between clean and unclean, in the ceremonies connected with leprosy and childbirth. It was not

[19] On the Sabbath, cf. R. North in *Biblica* (1955), 182–201. The "New Moon" is often mentioned among the traditional feasts: "New Moons, Sabbaths, assemblies, I will not tolerate your feasts and solemnities", Isa. 1.13; cf. 1 Sam. 20.5,18,27.

in Israel's character to philosophize about such
matters, but the essential character of their own
religion imposed itself on such primitive customs and used them to express deeper ideas
about "holiness".[20]

The all-pervading character of religion, as
well as Israel's traditionally patriarchal organization, meant that most of their religious practice
was essentially a domestic affair; it was not, in
other words, primarily a matter of "church-
going". But there were great communal occasions
of religious celebration, the great feasts. These
feasts were largely agricultural in character, and
were clearly not an original invention of the
Israelites; they were probably taken over from
the Canaanites along with the technique of
agriculture itself. The main feasts were the feast
of Unleavened Bread, celebrating the beginning
of the harvest by a meal of new corn; the feast of
"Weeks"—so called because it was determined
by a certain number of weeks from the first feast
—celebrating the end of the harvest; and the
feast of "Booths" (Tabernacles), celebrating the
grape-harvest, and probably so called because of
the custom of erecting shelters in the vineyard
during this period.

[20] Cf. Eichrodt, *Theology of the Old Testament*, vol.
1, 133–7.

Another feast, known as "Passover", was a survival from Israel's nomadic past; its main feature was the offering of a lamb in order to ensure the fertility of the flocks. This was a spring festival. Agricultural feasts, depending as they do on climate and weather, cannot be tied to any fixed date—the beginning of the harvest would vary from year to year and even from district to district. But since both Passover and Unleavened Bread were spring festivals they were eventually combined.

These feasts of the agricultural year were an essential part of pagan religion, which was a "nature religion". But it is characteristic of Israel that they were assimilated to their own religious ethos and transformed into a commemoration, not merely of the cycle of nature, but of the story of salvation. The spring festival, the combined Passover and Unleavened Bread, became the occasion for commemorating the beginning of their national existence, a commemoration of their deliverance at the Exodus (and even the ritual of the original feasts was interpreted in this sense: the garb and aspect of a semi-nomadic shepherd now expresses the preparation for flight; the sprinkling of the lamb's blood to ward off evil spirits now expresses their preservation from God's plague on the Egyptians; the unleavened bread now expresses the

5

hasty meal before departure). The Feast of Weeks was made the occasion for commemorating the giving of the Law at Sinai; and the Feast of Tabernacles commemorated the period of their "tent-dwelling" during the wandering in the desert. For the pagans, these feasts scanning the whole year link their lives to the cycle of nature. Israel had the same idea; the pattern of their lives which these annual feasts symbolized was seen to be determined by the great event of their deliverance by God, and the whole fabric of their lives was woven into the history of salvation.[21]

These feasts were celebrated at various local centres, such as Mizpah or Bethel. No doubt many of these shrines were taken over from the Canaanites, "holy places" which were legitimized by the tradition of an appearance of God to the Patriarchs in these places. (See p. 21.) Similarly,

[21] The reinterpretation of the Feast of Weeks, connecting it with the history of salvation, was probably a late development, in the last centuries of the Old-Testament era.

It is a view widely held today that Israel also celebrated a New-Year feast in honour of the enthronement of Yahweh, and that this is reflected in many of the Psalms (Ps. 93 is one example). Eichrodt, *Theology of the Old Testament*, vol. 1, 122–8, develops this theory and suggests a connection with the Feast of Tabernacles. For a balanced judgement on the theory see De Vaux, *Ancient Israel*, 502–506.

they took over from the Canaanites the custom of worshipping God at "high places", either actual hills or artificially constructed elevations which, reaching up to heaven, were considered suitable places for worship. The Babylonian *ziggurat* is based on this idea, and Jacob's dream reflects the same thought: the ladder pitched between earth and heaven is "the gate of heaven and the house of God". (Gen. 28.17.)

The principal act of worship was sacrifice. Sacrifices were offered on all religious occasions —not merely the great feasts, but the family and private occasions referred to above. The objects offered were naturally those in daily use in the people's own lives— domestic animals or birds, and secondarily corn, oil, wine and incense. The ritual differed with the different occasions, but in general there were three ways of treating the offering: either it was completely burnt, or part of it was burnt and part eaten, or merely the blood was sprinkled round the altar and the animal was then consumed in the normal way. Here again, as in the feasts, we can see a combination of different elements from different stages of Israel's development; those types of sacrifice in which blood plays a great part are similar to the sacrifices of the Arab tribes and probably derive from the nomadic period, whereas the others are more similar to Canaanite sacrifices and were adopted after the settlement.

In the significance attached to sacrifice we can again see the transformation of primitive ideas brought about by Israel's own theology. For example, the offering of a victim no doubt at one time represented a food or a bribe for the gods to appease their anger or to incline them to grant a request; but in Israelite thought it expressed self-surrender and recognition of God's dominion. Similarly, the eating of part of a victim at one time meant union with the god by means of some magical quality attached to the victim thus offered; but for Israel it represented community of mind and heart and life with their God.

The function of officiating at these ceremonies normally fell to the head of the family. This was certainly true in patriarchal times, and even at a later stage we find that private individuals like Gideon offer sacrifice (Judges 6.18), or that the king as head of the nation performs sacrificial acts.[22]

Priests too offered sacrifices; but the first function of the priests was the highly specialized skill of consulting the oracles. This was done by means of the Urim and Thummim. What exactly these were is not clear, but they must

[22] On the connection between kingship and priesthood, one may see *Witnesses to God*, 44f.

have been something like stones kept in a special
pouch (the ephod), to which a conventional value
was assigned so that they could provide the
answer to a properly phrased question. For
example, when David consulted Yahweh about
giving battle to the Philistines (1 Sam. 23.2), presumably it was decided beforehand that one
stone should have the value of an affirmative
answer and the other negative, so that the one
drawn out would provide the appropriate
answer. But this way of divining God's will
naturally declined in importance before the
Law, God's expressed will, and after the time
of David it is not heard of again. But the priests
were entrusted with a similar function in regard
to the Law. A body of basic principles was established very early in Israel's history—probably,
in fact, from the time of Sinai—but these principles had to be interpreted, and this was the
function of the priests. It was theirs to "judge
between clean and unclean" (Lev. 10.10), to
regulate the details of ritual, to apply the basic
commandments to particular cases. In fact, it
was out of such particular instructions that the
Law as we have it developed. But God's revelation was not confined to commands; it was
embodied in a history, and the priest's role as
teacher extended to this history also; when the
people gathered together, especially at the great

feasts, the story of God's great deeds was told, especially those relating to their own district, clan or shrine, and it was the priests who were responsible for this work too.

The priest, then, was the interpreter of God's will, the intermediary between God and man. Even in relation to sacrifice this was the role of the priests. They were not immolators, at least not primarily and by function. The immolation was normally performed by the person making the offering, and the priest's role was to offer it to God, placing it on the altar or sprinkling the blood.

Who were the priests? Many religious functions belonged normally to the head of the family; and when a permanent custodian was put in charge of some local sanctuary, it was open to anyone to perform this task. Samuel's parents, for example, belonged to the Tribe of Ephraim, but Samuel was brought up at the sanctuary of Shiloh and took on the priestly duties there. (1 Sam. 7.9 etc.) When the Ark was returned by the Philistines, the people of Kiriath-Jearim appointed Eleazar to its service simply because his family property provided a suitable site for it. (1 Sam. 7.1.) The priesthood was a job, more or less like any other; this is seen most clearly in the account of the sanctuary of Dan (Judges 17.4–18.26), where Micah first appoints his son to take charge of the shrine he has made for himself, and then offers the job to a casual passer-by: "Be my priest, and I will give you ten shekels of silver a year, clothing and food." (Judges 17.10.)

But as societies develop, functions tend to become specialized, especially those which involve some special secret or skill. This was certainly true of other professions, of which the secret was handed down from father to son; and it would be equally true of the priests. Gradually it came to be specialized in one tribe, the Tribe of Levi. Since the priest was attached to the shrine, the Tribe of Levi had no specific tribal territory.[23] But the office was not exclusive to members of this tribe, and the reign of Solomon itself provides an example of the appointment of a non-Levite to this office. David maintained two priests: Abiathar, who seems to have belonged to the priestly caste, and Zadok, of whose origins nothing is known. Abiathar's loyalty was suspect because of his support of Adonijah, so Solomon dismissed him and left Zadok in charge when the Temple was built.

[23] Another theory of the relationship between the priestly "levites" and the Tribe of Levi is that the name "levi" simply means "priest", as in the Minaean (South Arabian) dialect; and that this priestly caste took the place of the secular Tribe of Levi when the latter was almost wiped out in some unknown disaster, as is suggested by Gen. 49.5–7. Cf. Eichrodt, *Theology of the Old Testament*, vol. 1, 393–5.

The Temple of Solomon, then, was neither the first nor the only place of worship. At various places designated as holy, at high places, on altars of rough stone, the worship of God was carried on in the villages and tribes of Israel. But the prestige of the Temple gave it an attraction which far exceeded that of any other place of worship. It was under royal patronage, the priest was a royal official. The building itself was more magnificent than any other, the appointments more lavish (besides the great altar of sacrifice standing in front of the building, there was an altar of incense inside the main hall, a table on which a daily offering of bread was made, a magnificent ornate lamp-stand, and all the accessories of a great religious centre). The liturgy was performed there with unparalleled splendour; under the head priest there was a body of assistant clergy, and there were choirs trained by professional Canaanite musicians skilled in musical instruments and singing.[24] But most of all, it was the place where God dwelt. The Ark of the Covenant was there, the throne of God, so that the Temple was his palace. To go to the Temple was to go "before the face of Yahweh". He was not to be seen, but he was nevertheless really there, enthroned between the cherubs. Other shrines, other holy places, might be holy

[24] See above, p. 111, n. 13.

because they marked the scene of some visitation of God; but God did not merely appear in this place—here his name dwelt for ever. The Temple was the continuation of the Tent of the desert, the symbol of God's covenant presence, symbol of the Covenant itself by which God became "God with them", God in their midst, never-failing source of protection and strength.

Thus, though the monarchy conferred prestige on the Temple, it was even more true that the Temple conferred prestige on the monarchy. It marked the completion of David's work of identifying the dynasty with the Covenant. During the days of their wandering God had been present with them in the Tent; his presence now in the Temple signified his continuing presence in their settled state: and this settled state was summed up and symbolized in the monarchy.

## 10. The Administration of the State

Under Solomon's initiative the state of Israel grew in power and importance, and this called for a development also of the administrative machinery. The development may be illustrated by comparing it with the position under Saul and then under David. Saul has no officials at all, strictly speaking; there is merely a list of his

family, and among them it is mentioned that
Abner, his uncle, was in command of the army.
(1 Sam. 14.50.) (Excavation, too, confirms that
Saul's home-town, Gibeah, contained no very
lavish buildings.) David's court is much more
imposing; it consists of a commander-in-chief
of the army, a commander of the guard, a herald
and a secretary. (2 Sam. 8.15–18.) Solomon's is
much more developed still. (1 Kings 4.1–6.)

It included a priest, a commander-in-chief, a
major-domo, two secretaries, a herald, officers in
charge of the prefects and of levies, and a
"friend" of the king. The last is probably a
generic title, perhaps equivalent to "courtier"—
or perhaps something like "minister without
portfolio". The priest and the commander of the
army need no explanation. The position of
major-domo or master of the palace was originally a domestic office, concerned with the royal
household; but gradually it came to include the
charge of the whole administration, a position
second to that of the king himself. The secretary
was both private secretary to the king and secretary of state—responsible for the copying of
official correspondence and also for the form and
even for the contents. The herald similarly began
as a simple domestic official, for announcing the
names for audience and proclaiming royal

decisions; but he came to be the king's intermediary in his relations with the people.

The other two offices—the "charge of the prefects and the charge of the levies"—are connected with significant changes in Solomon's
administration of the country. The first office
is connected with a change in the system of taxation, by which the country was divided into
various districts, each under a prefect. The
second is connected with the introduction of
forced labour.

## 11. THE SEEDS OF DISCONTENT

But these last two offices draw our attention
to dangerous weaknesses in the structure of
Solomon's state. The first is an economic weakness. In spite of the vast wealth which flowed
into the country from trade, from duties and
from tribute from subject states, the magnificent
buildings and extravagant standard of living of
the court managed to outstrip this income.
Solomon was forced to cede twenty towns in the
north of the country to Hiram of Phoenicia in
return for cash. (1 Kings 9.10ff.) And the division
of the country into districts was another attempt
to meet the problem; each district was expected
to provide for the upkeep of the royal household
for one month every year.

This was a great burden on the people. But an even heavier burden was the duty of forced labour which Solomon introduced—and this, besides being a heavy financial burden, was in addition an unheard-of indignity. The use of slave labour was recognized in Israel—prisoners of war from defeated countries were used for this purpose, as we see in the case of David with the defeated Ammonites. (2 Sam. 12.31.) Solomon extended this practice to include also slaves drawn from the Canaanite sections of the population, whom he used in the mines at Ezion-Geber and in his merchant fleet. (1 Kings 9.20–21.) But finally Solomon found it necessary to extract the same service from free-born Israelites; and for the fierce independence of the tribes, especially with the memory of the slavery from which they had escaped to become a free people, this was a humiliation not easily borne.

But an even deeper source of discontent was Solomon's tactless disregard for tribal traditions. The administrative districts which he set up were a new departure in Israelite government, in that they cut across tribal territorial divisions. No doubt there were reasons of administrative convenience in this; or it is possible that it was a deliberate attempt to break down tribal loyalties in favour of the single centralized authority of the crown. But in either case, it was far too

premature, in striking contrast to the prudence
and caution with which David had moved in
building up the idea of the monarchy.

But at the same time as affronting tribal
loyalties, Solomon also managed to stress one
form of tribal distinction which it would have
been better to obliterate, and this was the distinction between northern and southern tribes.
David had taken great care not to let this division
go too far; this was in fact the great work of his
reign, to knit the scattered tribes into a unity.
For historical and geographical reasons there
tended to be a certain distance between the
northern and southern tribes, which became an
overt breach after the death of Saul. David
managed this situation very carefully; he refrained from imposing his authority on the
north by force, but let the split heal itself as
easily as possible. When it came to choosing his
capital he selected the neutral city of Jerusalem.
Even so, the division remained, a continual
ground of potential trouble; both the revolt of
Absalom (2 Sam. 15.1–5) and that of Sheba (2
Sam. 20.1–2) worked on this division. But now
Solomon, instead of working to obliterate this
dangerous division in the kingdom, almost gives
the impression of deliberately widening it. Jeroboam, for example, is said to have been in charge
of the labour force "of the House of Joseph" (1

Kings 11.29); it is not suggested that Judah was exempt, but at least it shows that a definite distinction was made between the two parts of the kingdom. Similarly, the administrative districts given in the text (1 Kings 4.8–19) cover only the north; again, it is not suggested that Judah was exempt—a brief note added to the list says that Judah had its own prefect, and it has been suggested that the list of towns in Joshua 15.21–62 is actually drawn from the division of the territory under the monarchy.[25] But once more, at the very least it means that the king was making a clear distinction between the status of the two parts of the nation.

The total picture of Solomon's reign, then, is mixed. On the surface—though not only on the surface—it was a picture of glittering success: with a few possible exceptions, his empire was as great as David had made it; the country had won a position of remarkable respect and influence and was undoubtedly the leading power in the Near East at that time; the prosperity of the country had increased manifold, and this showed its effect in the cultural life, in literature, music and notably in architecture. But at a deeper level, there was room for fore-

[25] Cf. F. M. Cross and G. E. Wright, "The Boundary and Province Lists of the Kingdom of Judah", *Journal of Biblical Literature* (1956), 202–226.

boding. There was abundant food for discontent, not least on the most important grounds of the relationship between the new regime and the basic patterns of the national life. By building the Temple in Jerusalem and housing there the Ark, Solomon had indeed seemed to be continuing and strengthening his father's policy of uniting Israel's essential religious traditions with this political form. But from a religious point of view, the stories of his laxity in observance (1 Kings 11.1–8) raised the suspicion that he did not appreciate as David had done the character and importance of the national faith; and from a political point of view, his methods do not lead us to believe that he appreciated the importance and the strength of the national traditions.

# THE DIVIDED KINGDOM

## 1. 931–853

SOLOMON thought himself strong enough to override any objection to his policy; and so he was; as long as the excitement of success continued, the people were willing to tolerate a great deal. But the objections were still there; and as soon as Solomon died they broke to the surface.

The spokesman for the protests was Jeroboam. He had been an overseer of a forced-labour party drawn from the northern tribes, but he had plotted rebellion, and when this was discovered he had taken refuge in Egypt. A new dynasty had come to power there, displacing that with which Solomon was connected by marriage; and in any case Solomon was not prepared to make an issue of this very minor affair of an unimportant troublemaker. But after Solomon's death, Jeroboam returned and led a deputation to the new king, Solomon's son Rehoboam.

The immediate object of this representation was mild and reasonable—relief from taxation. But young men of Rehoboam's generation, brought up knowing only the absolutism of Solomon's court, did not realize the significance of this popular representation, and chose to regard it as mere insolence. And when this request was refused, the deeper sources of resentment sprang to the surface. The cry that was then raised is significant: "To your tents, O Israel: what have we to do with the House of David?" What was at stake was not merely the matter of taxation, or even the more general question of social justice; what lay behind this was a deeper grievance, the traditional antagonism of the north against the south. And the result this time was secession and the formation of a separate state.

## 1. THE FIRST YEARS

Rehoboam did not at first grasp the full gravity of the situation, and continued to treat it merely as an isolated act of rebellion—to treat it as David had treated the rebellion of Absalom or of Sheba. But his attempts to enforce submission were roundly defeated, and the situation degenerated into a matter of local battles concerned mainly with boundaries. The position of Benjamin between north and south was particularly open to doubt, and was particularly important since Jerusalem lay within this territory.

Rehoboam did in fact hold Jerusalem, but the demarcation line between the two opposing states was never formally fixed; it was probably a *de facto* boundary based on the outcome of these local battles (Jericho, for example, belonged to the northern kindom, whereas Aijalon, though more or less on a level with it, belonged to the south).

But in any case, any hope that Judah may have had of bringing the north quickly back to obedience was decisively ended by an invasion from Egypt. The Libyan king who had come to power there,[1] Shishak, seems to have had some thought of restoring Egypt's previous control over Palestine. It was he who had harboured Jeroboam, and now that Solomon's empire was showing signs of weakening he was able to take direct action. Traces of the invasion have been found as far north as Megiddo (where he set up a victory stele), and the Bible reports the crippling tribute that Judah was forced to pay. Fortunately Shishak's own position in Egypt was not sufficiently secure to permit him to carry his plans further; his forces withdrew and Rehoboam

---

[1] Egypt never really recovered from the weakness brought about by the invasion of the Peoples of the Sea, but Libyan or Ethiopian kings occasionally seized power and this infusion of new blood sparked off efforts to regain Egypt's former empire in Palestine.

built a line of forts along his southern border to guard against any future attack. But both Judah and Israel were sufficiently shocked by the experience to put an end to their own fighting for the time being.

## 2. THE BIRTH-PANGS OF THE NORTH

If Rehoboam had sought historical precedent for his position, he might have taken encouragement from the experience of his grandfather David. For although the defection of the northern tribes was now seen to be something more than an easily suppressed revolt like that of Absalom, nevertheless, he might have thought, it was not unlike the situation at the beginning of David's reign, when for seven years the northern tribes refused him their allegiance.

But if he had then thought back a little further—to the time of Saul—he might have begun to wonder whether it was the central monarchy rather than the rebellion which was the temporary phenomenon. David had made the monarchy acceptable; Solomon had made it glorious; yet here within the space of a century the situation was back to something very like what it had been before.

For the most fundamental cause of the rebellion of the northern tribes—deeper than

*The Divided Kingdom*

| Judah | | Israel | Others |
|---|---|---|---|
| Rehoboam | 930 | Jeroboam I | Shishak of Egypt |
| Abijam | | Nadab | |
| Asa | 900 | Baasha | Ben Hadad I of Damascus |
| | 890 | Elah | |
| | | Zimri | |
| | 880 | Omri | |
| Jehoshaphat | 870 | Ahab | Ben Hadad II |
| | | | Shalmaneser III |
| | 850 | Ahaziah | Battle of Qarqar, 853 |
| Jehoram | | Jehoram | |
| Ahaziah | | | |
| Athaliah | 840 | Jehu | |
| Joash | | | |
| | 830 | | |
| | 820 | | |
| | | Jehoahaz | |
| | 810 | | |
| Amaziah | 800 | Jehoash | |
| | 790 | | |
| | | Jeroboam II | |
| Uzziah | 780 | | |
| | | (*Amos*) | |
| | 770 | (*Hosea*) | |
| | 760 | | |
| | 750 | | |
| | | Zechariah | Tiglath Pileser III |
| Jotham (*Isaiah*) | 740 | Shallum | |
| Ahaz    (*Micah*) | | Menahem | |
| | 730 | Pekahiah | |
| | | Pekah | |
| | 721 | Hoshea | |
| Hezekiah | 700 | | |
| Manasseh | | | |
| Amon | 650 | | |
| Josiah | | | |
| (*Jeremiah*) | | | |
| Jehoahaz | 600 | | Nebuchadnezzar |
| Jehoiakim | | | |
| Jehoiachin | | | |
| Zedekiah | 587 | | |

*The history of the divided kingdom is so fragmented that any detailed treatment would be confusing. This chapter tries to present a coherent picture through the main events, and this chart may assist the reader to situate these events in the general history of the time.*

bureaucratic oppression, deeper than the jealousy
of north and south, deeper even than tribal independence—was that question of principle
which had dogged the monarchy from the beginning: "They have rejected me, Yahweh, as
their king." (1 Sam. 8.7.) This was not merely
impractical religious idealism which sought to
uphold a strict theocracy. Here, as always in the
history of Israel, politics and religion cannot be
separated. What was at stake was the social and
political form which was permissible to them in
virtue of their essential constitution, which was
the covenant with God. It was the Covenant
which made them a people. To adopt a mon-
archical system, it was thought, would be to
transfer the focal point of the nation to the king;
the whole life of the state would revolve round
him, he would be the principle of unity, he
would be the source of law, the prosperity of the
nation would depend on him. And in these
conditions what would become of the Covenant?
Instead of being twelve tribes welded into one
by the common covenant with God, Israel
would be simply a state united by the authority
of the king.

David had shown that this need not be so; he
had shown that the King of Israel would not
displace the Covenant but would embody it. But
Solomon, in the eyes of many, in the north

particularly, had seemed to go beyond this acceptable development and to be moving in the direction of a purely secular autocracy. And it was against this that the protest was aimed; against secular autocracy in favour of an older, more democratic ideal which was at the same time felt to be more in accordance with the character of the Covenant People.[2]

But such a train of thought called into question the very principle of authority. Once David's dynasty was rejected, there was no particular reason why Jeroboam's should be accepted. The rebellion was an attempt to return to an older ideal; but in practice the older situation had been one of near-anarchy on which the nation had almost foundered. It was not unexpected, therefore, that the same sort of situation should appear now in the northern kingdom.

The momentum of revolt maintained Jeroboam's authority during his own lifetime; but

[2] Such a protest, combining a protest against tyranny with a religious, theocentric concern, is in accordance with the prophetic tradition; and it seems possible that the Prophets may have played some part in fostering the rebellion. It was the prophet Ahijah of Shiloh—the old covenant centre of the tribes—who first encouraged Jeroboam. (1 Kings 11.29–40.) On the other hand, this same Ahijah later condemned Jeroboam because he was "not like David". (1 Kings 14.8ff.) No doubt contemporary opinion was a confused mixture of religious, political and anti-monarchic sentiment.

his son Nadab reigned for only two years before being assassinated by one of his army officers called Baasha. This established a precedent; Baasha's son Ela was assassinated in his turn, and the usurper, Zimri, lasted only one week.

## 3. THE ARAMEANS

These internal difficulties were complicated by the international situation at that time. Under David and especially under Solomon, Israel had more than held its own in the world; but the inevitable and immediate result of the division of the kingdom was to reduce the great state of David and Solomon to the rank of two minor states of no greater size or importance than any of the other minor states around them; and the former subjects of the empire were now a threat to Israel's security. The greatest threat came from the Arameans.

The Arameans were probably a branch of the same semi-nomadic family of peoples from which Israel itself was descended.[3] According to Israelite tradition both Aram and Heber are "sons of Shem" (Gen. 10.22f), and Deuteronomy can put into the mouth of an Israelite, "My father

[3] For earlier references to the Arameans, see *ANET*, 275; and on the Arameans generally, A. Dupont-Sommer, *Les Araméens* (1948).

was a wandering Aramean." (Deut. 26.5.) Jacob, in particular (Gen. 24.10:28.5), is connected with a region in which the name "Aram" occurs —Paddan-Aram or Aram-Naharaim.

During the great period of semi-nomadic migrations with which this history opened, the tribes from whom the Arameans were descended remained in Mesopotamia; but their great period of expansion came after the disruption caused by the Peoples of the Sea in the thirteenth century. They swarmed in on the territory of the defeated Hittites and Mitanni, strong enough to bar the expansion of Assyria. They spread down the Euphrates and to the west, so that by the eleventh century numerous Aramean states were established from Babylon to Damascus.

But this was precisely the period in which David was expanding his empire, and a clash between the two was almost inevitable. But this clash, when it came, illustrates a curious characteristic of the Arameans—their inability to unite in a single empire; indeed, the various Aramean states were almost as likely to be at war with each other as with any outside power. Thus, when the Ammonites call on the Arameans for help, it is on individual states that they call—the Arameans of Zobah and the Arameans of Rehob. (2 Sam. 10.6.) And when David turns on the Arameans after his defeat of the Ammonites, the Aramean

King of Hamath expresses his gratitude for David's defeat of his neighbour, Zobah. (2 Sam. 8.9–10.) It appears that the King of Zobah was trying to do for the Arameans what David did for the Israelites—to draw them into a union strong enough to form a great empire. He managed to form a coalition of the states around Zobah, and was trying to extend his influence "beyond the river", beyond the Euphrates; but at least one of his neighbours did not find this prospect to his liking.

David forced these states to recognize his sovereignty, and Solomon continued to exercise authority there; but his power was not undisputed. A certain Rezon made himself ruler of Damascus, and declared his independence of Israel. How much trouble he was able to cause Solomon we do not know; but the division of the kingdom after Solomon's death was clearly his opportunity.

Fighting between Israel and Judah flared up again when Abijam, Rehoboam's son, advanced into Israel. At first he was successful and even forced Jeroboam to move his capital from Shechem to Penuel beyond the Jordan. But the Israelites reacted strongly, and in desperation Judah called on Damascus for help. The King of Damascus was naturally delighted to comply with this request; and thereafter not only regarded the Israelites as fair game for armed raid, but even began to annexe some of their territory.

This was an important factor in Israel's lack of internal stability. These military reverses caused dissatisfaction, especially in the army, and led to the series of assassinations already described; and this, coupled with the theological uncertainty dealt with above, brought the country to a pitch of unrest and anarchy in which the disintegration of the state seemed imminent. And it was in these conditions that Omri came to power.

## 4. OMRI

Omri was a general who was brought to power, like his immediate predecessors, by the army's discontent. But he showed himself more than merely a military dictator. He is the real founder of the state of Israel. Up till his time, it had been a province in revolt, not too sure of itself nor of where it was going. It was Omri who established the fact that it was to be an independent state.

One sign of this new beginning was the building of a new capital. Jeroboam had set up his headquarters first at Shechem and then at Penuel, and Baasha had moved back across the

Jordan and made Tirzah his centre. Now Omri built a new city at Samaria. The choice was dictated by motives similar to those which had led David to choose Jerusalem—its central position and its freedom from association with the previous troubled history. And like Jerusalem, this capital too was dignified with splendid buildings and works of art reflecting the stability and prosperity which Omri brought to the country.

Stability and security—Omri was quick to see that these were the first and most important needs if his state was to survive; and he was quick to see too that these could not be achieved by Israel struggling alone—caught between two dangerous enemies, Judah to the south and the Arameans to the north, her need for external support and alliance was imperative. For this purpose, he turned to Solomon's old ally, Phoenicia. This was particularly appropriate, for Ittobaal, the King of Phoenicia, had himself recently seized power, and the two usurpers were able to lend each other mutual support. The alliance was sealed by marriage between Omri's son Ahab and the Tyrian princess Jezebel. Evidence of the economic advantage of the alliance can be seen in the ivory plaques of Phoenician workmanship which have been found in Samaria.

But an even greater diplomatic triumph for Omri was the alliance with Judah. Jehoshaphat, King of Judah, realized that there was nothing to be gained now by pursuing an ancient feud; the existence of the northern state was a *fait accompli*, and negotiations were carried on not as with a rebellious subject but as with an independent state of equal status. This alliance too was accompanied by closer family ties, marriage between Jehoshaphat's son Jehoram and Omri's daughter.[4]

The state of Israel was now firmly established for the first time since it broke away from the House of David. It was not to be expected that the ravages of the previous years should be automatically reversed—we know, for example, that Omri was forced to cede some territory to the Aramean King of Damascus. But gradually the effect did show. It showed during the reign of Omri himself, when he brought the Moabites back into subjection; but it showed even more strikingly in the time of his son Ahab, in a

[4] According to 2 Kings 8.18 and 2 Chron. 21.6, Athaliah was the daughter of Ahab, therefore granddaughter of Omri. According to 2 Kings 8.26 and 2 Chron. 22.2, she was Omri's daughter. It is not certain when the marriage took place, but since it seems, like the marriage of Ahab and Jezebel, to be the outcome of Omri's political activities, it seems more probable that Athaliah was Omri's daughter.

surprise victory over the Arameans. Having met
with so little opposition in the preceding years,
the Arameans were now in a position to threaten
even the capital, Samaria; and Ahab felt that the
time had come to resist. So unexpected was his
success in this encounter that the Arameans
blamed it on lack of support from their allies
and on the fact that the battle had been fought
in mountainous terrain in which the Israelites
were notoriously skilful. But the next year Ben
Hadad of Damascus returned to the attack in
conditions more favourable to himself, and once
more the Israelites were completely victorious,
and Ben Hadad himself was taken prisoner.

Ahab's conduct then at first sight looks like
incredible folly, and certainly there were many
in Israel who thought so, and criticized Ahab
severely for it. He treated his defeated enemy
with astonishing leniency. Instead of dealing out
the expected death penalty, he welcomed Ben
Hadad as a friend and formed an alliance with
him.

But the true explanation for this apparent
weakness is to be found in an even greater danger
which at that moment overshadowed both Israel
and Aram alike. This danger was the rising
power of Assyria.

## 5. ASSYRIA

A trading nation in northern Mesopotamia, known in history as far back as the second millennium, Assyria had up till now shown little inclination to imperial power—and in any case had been in no position to achieve it, hemmed in by a succession of vigorous nations, Hittites, Mitanni and now the Arameans. But during all this time Assyria had been steadily growing in strength and now a ruthless fighting force was prepared which was to dominate the history of the Near East for the next two centuries.

The first step was to secure her borders at home. First the pillaging tribes to the east were brought into subjection, and then the little Aramean states round the Euphrates. But then the Assyrian armies began to range further and further afield; Ashur-nasir-pal II (883–859), for example, campaigned as far as the Mediterranean—winning himself a reputation for brutality, in a nation notorious for its cruelty, by his burning, slaughtering, pillaging and deporting.

At first these campaigns against the other Aramean states merely left Damascus all the more free to extend her power, with the effects that we have seen on the kingdoms of Israel and Judah. But now, under Shalmaneser III

(858–824), the Assyrian advance grew closer and more terrifying, and the smaller nations realized that their only hope of survival lay in combining all their forces. A coalition was formed under the leadership of Damascus and Israel, and battle was joined at Qarqar in 853. The Assyrian account of this battle claims a great victory[5]; but the fact that it was several years before they ventured west again shows that the coalition was at least partly successful.

This set the pattern for the next few years. Whenever there was a threat of invasion from Assyria the smaller nations sank their differences to face the danger; but as soon as the immediate danger was averted hostilities between them were once more renewed. The position of Assyria is the key to the fluctuating relationships between Israel and Damascus which in the Bible appear so haphazard and confused.

So at this time also, when the Battle of Qarqar had achieved its purpose in halting the Assyrians, Israel resumed hostilities against Damascus. Encouraged by his previous successes, Ahab now tried to drive the Arameans from Israelite territory altogether. With his ally, Jehoshaphat, King of Judah, he marched against the frontier town of Ramoth Gilead, then in the hands of

[5] For the Assyrian account of the battle, see *ANET*, 277–9.

Damascus. This time, however, he was less successful. Ahab himself lost his life in the battle; and the campaign then dragged on for another eight years, to the increasing exasperation of the people.

### 6. REACTION AGAINST THE OMRIDES

This exasperation was increased by developments which had taken place in the religious situation. The rebellion against the dynasty of David was not intended to signal desertion of the national religion—indeed it was intended to be a blow struck in defence of the Covenant against the encroachments of monarchy. But David's dynasty had already become so identified with the covenant faith that the rebellion was bound to bring about religious difficulties. The difficulty was pinpointed in the position of Jerusalem. This was not merely an enemy capital; it was the site of the Temple, the shrine of the Ark, the focal point of the Covenant. Jeroboam tried to counter this by setting up two national shrines of his own—one at Bethel, which claimed association with the Patriarchs, and the other at Dan in the north, which was given a certain standing by the presence of clergy descended from Moses himself. (Judges 18.30.)

In these shrines he set up golden bulls. It seems probable that these were not idols nor even symbols of Yahweh, but merely pedestals on which God was enthroned. Other gods at the time are pictured thus, standing on the figure of a bull[6]; and the fact that here the bulls alone were represented suggests that the thought was really essentially the same as that concerning the Ark in the Jerusalem Temple—Yahweh was *invisibly* enthroned; these bulls, in other words, were merely the equivalent of the cherubs in the inner shrine of the Temple. But it is true that the bull was closely associated with the pagan fertility cult, and the ordinary Israelite, and even more, the large numbers of Canaanites in the northern kingdom, could not be expected to distinguish very carefully.

But the danger was vastly increased through Israel's alliance with Tyre. It was not merely that Jezebel continued to worship her own god Baal after her marriage to Ahab, and that a temple to this god was built in Samaria; Solomon too had permitted his wives to continue on Israelite soil the worship of the gods of the lands from which they came; but this was a purely domestic matter, and while it was not a course which any earnest follower of Yahweh would

[6] Such figures can be seen, for example, in *The Ancient Near East in Pictures*, 163–70.

6

approve, it did not at all imply apostasy. But Jezebel was a strong-minded and overbearing woman, and she took active steps to introduce the worship of Baal on a national scale. In this she may have been moved by genuine religious zeal for her god, but it was also at least partly national pride—the triumph of her god was the triumph of her people, a sign of the cultural and political superiority of Tyre. The incident of Naboth's vineyard (1 Kings 21) is significant in this connection. When Naboth refused to sell his vineyard to Ahab, the king, however grudgingly, had to recognize his rights; Jezebel, however, simply had the man put to death. This was typical of the despotism which was normal in other monarchies of the day, from which Israel was saved by the law of Yahweh, to which the king too was subject. But for Jezebel this was an intolerable limitation of the royal authority, and her action shows her contempt both for Israel's religion and for Israel's political system; she was determined to raise the monarchy to the status it enjoyed in her own country, at the expense of the religion which would limit it.

Once again, the ordinary Israelite could not be expected to realize all that was at stake, especially when the new religion was propagated with all the authority and influence of the government behind it; while for the Canaanites, this was merely a return to their traditional customs which they had never really left.

But there were others who did realize what was at stake—who realized that since Yahweh alone is God, the worship of Baal was not just a harmless variant or permissible political expedient. Chief among these was Elijah, an ascetic, hermit-like figure who came out of seclusion to wage a private war for Yahweh against the government, for Yahweh's law against the whims of rulers. It is a tribute to his influence that his story is inserted at this point in the Bible (1 Kings 17–21) in preference to ordinary political history.

But Jezebel was not the woman to submit meekly to his rebukes. She intensified her efforts, her positive persecution of the old faith, and Elijah himself was eventually forced to take refuge from her vengeance (and it is significant that it was to Horeb that he fled, the place where the Yahwist faith had begun). But he had done his work; he had roused the national conscience, and a growing body of opinion in the country— the groups of devout men known as "the Sons of the Prophets", for example, or the ascetic clan of Rechab (2 Kings 10.15; Jer. 25.1–11)—was stirred to active resentment. This religious feeling combined with other factors—the despotism of the regime and its ineptness in the Aramean war—and finally burst out in violence.

Elijah himself, seeing no hope of reform from any member of Ahab's family, took steps to overthrow the dynasty. He sent one of his followers, Elisha, to Jehu, the general in charge of operations at Ramoth Gilead (see p. 151), to declare that it was Yahweh's will that he should take over the kingship. Jehu was then acclaimed by the army, and immediately set out for Jezreel, where the king had established his headquarters. Jehu at once struck down the king, Jehoram, with his own hand. Ahaziah, King of Judah was also there—the alliance between the two states was still in effect and they had joined forces again for this campaign—and by his presence he was considered to be implicated in the guilt of Ahab's family, and he too was assassinated. Next it was the turn of Jezebel herself, thrown to her death from the window of her palace. Then Jehu set about a complete purge of the old regime—the rest of the royal family, the court, and finally a wholesale massacre of devotees of Baal assembled in the temple of Baal in Samaria. One may hesitate to say that the religion of Yahweh had conquered by such bloody means, but certainly Baal was defeated.

## 7. EVENTS IN JUDAH

Events in Judah followed on a minor scale the same pattern as those in Israel. The division of the kingdom destroyed the power of both states. Judah was left open to attack from the south, just as Israel was from the north; but the danger from Egypt was never as acute as that from the Arameans. Judah lost control of the Philistines and Edomites, as Israel had of the Moabites. But the alliance with Israel which Omri instigated brought strength to both states, and Jehoshaphat of Judah was able to regain control of the Philistine territory and to subdue the Edomites. This latter in turn enabled him to renew Solomon's trading policy from Ezion Geber. The security which followed also gave him the opportunity to institute internal reforms, in particular the reform of the judicial system (2 Chron. 19.8–11); the system by which the king acted as court of appeal to the locally elected courts had grown too unwieldy, and Jehoshaphat set up a supreme court under the priests for religious affairs and a royal minister for civil affairs.

But—again as in Israel—this success was only temporary; under Jehoram the Philistines rebelled once more, control of Edom was lost (and with it the loss of the port and mines of Ezion Geber); and above all, Judah was associated with Israel in the ill-fated Aramean war. And in Judah too, as in Israel, the political dissatisfaction thus engendered combined with religious forces to bring about a change of government.

Paganism never made such great inroads in Judah as it did in Israel, but the danger was always there, and the kings were not always energetic in countering it. Jehoshaphat did make some effort to control it; but on the other hand, his alliance with Israel and intermarriage with Omri's family gave paganism official entry into the country. Athaliah was a woman of the same stamp as Jezebel, and when her son Ahaziah fell in Jehu's purge, she seized power herself. She wiped out all the rest of the royal family, with the exception of one child, Joash, who was saved by one of the priests. She then tried, as Jezebel had in the north, to transform Judah into a pagan state subject to a despotic monarchy. But the situation in Judah was not the same as it was in Israel; for one thing, paganism was not so widespread in the south as it was in the north, with its large Canaanite population; and moreover, Judah had a tradition of stability and loyalty to the Davidic dynasty which the north lacked. So it did not need fiery prophetic denunciation and violent action to bring about the fall of Athaliah. The priests had only to bring forward the boy Joash at a suitable moment for the people to rally to his support and depose Athaliah. She was put to death, and for a few years at least there was a revival of the traditional faith.

## 2. 853–721

### 1. A PERIOD OF PROSPERITY

In spite of the dramatic changes in internal events which put a decisive end to the previous period, external events at first showed no improvement. The accession of the general, Jehu, in Israel, occasioned partly by the army's impatience, might have seemed to promise a more vigorous conduct of the war against the Arameans. But in fact, things at first went even worse. The Arameans not only held Ramoth Gilead but even resumed the offensive. Soon the whole of Transjordan was in their hands, and then they forced their way down the Mediterranean coast as far as Philistia, and extracted crippling tribute from Judah also.

An accidental change in the international situation brought about a sudden and complete transformation. For a moment, Assyria regained power sufficiently to turn attention to the west once more; this period of Assyrian power lasted only twenty years, but in the course of it Damascus was so badly weakened that it was in no position to continue the offensive against Israel and Judah. The effect on Israel was evident almost immediately. The Arameans were driven out of Israelite territory, and even as far north as Hamath the Israelites waged victorious war.

Judah, too, shared in this success, and set about restoring her authority over the neighbouring peoples. The result was that the combined kingdoms of Jeroboam II of Israel and Uzziah of Judah were almost equal to the empire of Solomon. And the prosperity of the kingdoms, too, was such as the country had not known since the days of Solomon. Agriculture and industry flourished, and with the trade routes north in the hands of Israel and those south in the hands of Judah, wealth flowed in from all sides.

But the prosperity of this period showed itself most clearly in the abuses it brought forth. The splendid buildings and luxurious standards of living were paid for not only in wealth, but in oppression and injustice. Indeed, our knowledge of this period is largely due to the condemnations it called forth from the great prophets of the time—Amos and Hosea in the north, Micah and Isaiah in the south.

## 2. THE PROPHETS

Israel's religion was by now well organized. It had taken on an institutional character, with established forms, a body of laws, and regulating officials, priests and king. But behind all this there was a quality in Israel's religion which the institutions could not adequately express. An institution is of its nature conservative; it expresses and maintains the *status quo*. But at the very heart of Israelite religion there was a belief in a living God, one who acts and intervenes in history. It was such an unlooked-for intervention which lay at the very origin of their existence and their faith; and it was of the nature of such a God that he should be continually acting, continually breaking forth and breaking through the institution.

Thus, besides the role of the officials, a prominent part is played in Israel's history by men who act not in virtue of powers officially vested in them by the institution, but in virtue of the spirit of God which moves them. Such were the Judges, and such also were the *nebiim*[7] who

[7] *Nebiim*, plural of *nabi*, is used rather than "prophet", because our idea of what a "prophet" is is liable to be prejudiced by preconceived associations; whereas the section that follows tries to show that the phenomenon summed up in the word "prophecy" is not as simple as

appear at the time of the Philistine oppression and during the divided monarchy. The most evident external characteristic of these men is group ecstasy, accompanied often by dancing and music. (1 Sam. 10.5–10.) Similar phenomena occur in other civilizations also, and from this point of view the *nebiim* could no doubt be classed with the priests of Cybele, the dervishes of Islam, or, to come nearer home, the prophets of Baal in Canaan. (Cf. 1 Kings 18.26–8.) But without denying the force of such parallels, it must not be overlooked that the activity of the *nebiim* was not simply a manifestation of mass hysteria, nor a matter of extravagant personal devotion. Their activity is closely linked with the national religion. They are frequently associated with the national shrines, and the message they give is a recall to the God of Israel and a protest against the dangers which threaten this faith. This is to be seen in Nathan's rebuke of David (2 Sam. 12.1ff) or Elijah's rebuke of Ahab (1 Kings 21.17ff); these are not primarily the actions of courageous individualists against unjust authority, but protests against the flouting of Israel's religious ideals. The same close association between the *nebiim* and Israel's traditional

---

may be thought. On the Prophets, see B. Vawter, *The Conscience of Israel* (1961).

faith is to be seen in the emergence of the Elohist document of the Pentateuch.[8] The great work of J did not exhaust the whole repertoire of Israelite traditions, nor did it present the only possible view of them; and the prophets of the north, particularly, made use of another version of these traditions in their campaign. One can imagine these men going round among the people or addressing them as they gathered at the shrines on religious festivals, rallying their failing courage under the Philistines or their faltering faith under Jezebel, by these accounts of God's great deeds of old.

But although we must not merely dismiss this phenomenon as a rather suspect intrusion of Canaanite ways into Israel, it is true that it did contain the seeds of future decadence. The very success of the movement gave these seeds growth. Success brought prestige, and prestige brought self-seeking. Because these men were thought to be possessed by the spirit, they were regarded with awe and reverence; but when the spirit failed—as sometimes it must, for the spirit is not to be bound—how hard it was to forgo that reverence, and how easy to feign the ecstatic

[8] On this work (referred to by the initial E), see p. 111f. on J, and cf. A. Weiser, *Introduction to the Old Testament*, 110–25; Robert and Feuillet, *Introduction à la Bible*, vol. 1 362–7.

phenomena which were the sign of the spirit! The Bible tells us of groups of prophets; at best, this could be confraternities of devout men lending each other mutual support and infecting each other with their enthusiasm; but it could easily degenerate into almost professional bodies in which acquired skills—the skill of acting a prophet's part—were handed on. The words of the *nabi* were listened to even by kings; but there was the temptation to preserve the respect of princes by speaking the word which their hearers wished to hear. This is well illustrated in the incident in 1 Kings 22.1–28, where a band of 400 prophets was attached to the court and played the part of courtiers in assuring Ahab of victory in the coming battle. Instead of protesting, they have become conformists; instead of countering the rigidity of the institution by the dynamism of the spirit, they have been assimilated by the institution.

But when this type of *nabi* fell into disrepute, the movement itself took on new and more vigorous life in men of a different stamp.[9] The

---

[9] It may be objected that the first of this new type of prophet dissociates himself vehemently from the old class of *nabi*: "No *nabi* I, no son of a *nabi*." (Amos 7.14.) But this is primarily a disclaimer of the professionalism which had overtaken the prophetic guilds, not a denial that he belongs to the same general tradition.

ecstatic element was much less prominent in such men, though it was not altogether absent, as can be seen in the accounts of the calls of Isaiah and Jeremiah, and especially in Ezekiel. The strange symbolic deeds, by which men possessed by the spirit acted out the spirit's action, still played some part in their activity; but it was unhesitatingly subordinated to the gift of understanding and conveying God's message in intelligible words. The phenomenon of group ecstasy was completely absent; the individuality and even isolation of these figures was striking.

But these external differences were only the outward sign of a difference in their message; and it is the content of their message which makes it clear that a new spiritual force has made its way into Israelite history. Each of the prophets has his own message; but underlying all differences we can see a certain community of attitude.

Most fundamental of all is their startling awareness of God himself—his might, his supreme majesty, his total dominion, the infinite distance between him and all that is not God. This of course had been implicit in Yahwism from the begining; but in the first place, one may question how many had actually appreciated it; and in the second place, developments which had taken place since then had tended to obscure it. The idea of the divine "otherness" was common to other religions too, but in contemporary paganism it was confused by the idea of an arbitrary god who had to be controlled by a religion of "techniques".[10] Israel had come into close contact with the fertility-cult in Canaan, and had not escaped the danger of then treating their own religion as a matter of technique by which the Almighty could be manipulated. To this must be added the organization of the state religion. This state and this religion were of divine ordinance; but from this article of faith it was an easy step to the thought that God was tied down to the nation, to the Covenant, to the monarchy, to the Temple. The Prophets were not iconoclasts; but their vision of God was so much at variance with what religion had become that they could not but rise up to smash these idols which disguised and distorted the true nature of God.

This God, moreover, is a person; he is not to be equated with an impersonal force of nature, nor even kept comfortably at a distance as a national talisman. It is not sufficient to say that he is a moral God; Israel already knew him as the God of a moral law. But the Prophets saw even more clearly that this moral order was not a series of impersonal rules, but the expression of a

[10] Cf. L. Johnston, "Jeremiah and Morality", *Clergy Review* (1962), 142–7.

personal will. God is a person, real, living and terrifyingly close to each individual. Terrifying, for such a God is bound to run counter to all purely human ideals. When he speaks to men, it is not "comfortable words" that he speaks; what takes place is an irruption and disruption of human ways as destructive as that of a natural cataclysm.

But this does not mean that he is only a God of terror. His anger is only the result of an even deeper quality of his personality, and that is his love. It was because he loved Israel that he chose them—"It was not because you were great that he chose you, but simply because he loved you" (Deut. 7.8)—and because he loved them he would not easily let them reject him, to their own loss. The God of Israel is a jealous God. Just as his commandments are not impersonal rules, so his love is not detached benevolence, but includes a quality of personal involvement which Hosea does not hesitate to describe in terms of marital relationship: " I will allure her, and bring her into the wilderness and speak tenderly to her" (Hos. 2.14): "In that day, you will call me: 'My husband'. . . I will espouse you to myself for ever, I will espouse you in justice and right, in tenderness and love." (Hos. 2.16–19.)

But this heightened sense of the personal character and relationship with God did not make religion a private matter between God and the individual only. The Prophets realized that the dimensions of God's action are the whole of creation and the whole of time. It was against this background that they saw even his covenant with Israel; and this is the meaning of the political activity of the Prophets—they were indeed concerned with the national destiny and in particular with the dynasty of David (it was a prophetic oracle which sanctioned the founding of the dynasty, and prophets like Isaiah still see it as the source of national greatness); but it was not for the sake of the nation or the dynasty, but because through them God's dominion would be realized. And it is here that the prophetic awareness of God showed itself most terribly. Their awareness of God involved an awareness of sin that went far beyond formal recognition of individual transgressions. They saw that what was at stake was not just this or that sin, but a total inversion of the right order. God was being made subject to man; Israel was the People of God in the sense that she was the instrument of his will; but Israel looked on him as "our God", instrument of the national success and prosperity.

It was in the light of such principles that the Prophets saw the real meaning of events in Israel at this time, and saw, too, their inevitable outcome; they saw the rottenness underneath the present prosperity and the dissolution to which it was hastening.

The institution of the monarchy had imposed a certain strain on the covenant system; and the vast expansion of state administration under Solomon had increased the gap between the old order and the new, and laid the foundations of an aristocracy. The Canaanite influence of Omri's time had then made this distinction between ruler and ruled a recognized feature of the structure of the state. So that by the time of Jeroboam II there was an established class-distinction completely alien to the original covenant confraternity, and one which led to even more serious economic differences. This was a period of great prosperity; but the wealth was concentrated in the hands of a prosperous upper class, while the situation of the artisan and small farmer became even more desperate. Since they lacked any financial security, any minor setback (such as the drought which Amos refers to, Amos 4.7–9) forced them to seek a loan from the rich merchants—but the security for this loan was the land and even the life of the poor—". . . buying the poor for money and the needy for a pair of sandals". (Amos 8.6.) Not content with this, the rich increased their advantage by dishonest practices (Amos 8.5); nor was there any redress at law for the poor, for the courts themselves were corrupt. (Amos 5.7.)

In the circumstances, religious practices were shown up for what they were—a hollow mockery, a superstitious ritual devoid of real meaning. (Amos 5.21–4.) It was not a matter of conscious hypocrisy, but, what was even worse, of unconscious perversion. They no longer knew of what a God they were the people; therefore, said the prophets, they had forfeited the right to be the People of God. (Amos 9.7.)

### 3. FALL OF SAMARIA

The prophets' words are borne out by the suicidal frenzy which seems to grip the nation, like a mortally wounded beast tearing itself to pieces. The corruption which had spread through the whole body finally undermined the very structure of society and brought about a state of anarchy worse than that which had existed at the beginning. Jeroboam II's son Zechariah reigned for six months before his throne was seized by Shallum; he lasted a month, and then Menahem forced his way to power in a bloody civil war. He was succeeded by his son Pekahiah, but almost immediately he fell to another of the same name, Pekah.

And as if to give the death-stroke, Assyria now

appeared once more. Since the Battle of Qarqar
in 853, Assyria had been too occupied nearer
home to play any great part in affairs in Syria
and Palestine. Occasional raids did continue
after that, and in one brief period of aggression
at the beginning of the eighth century Damascus
was sufficiently curbed to allow Israel to achieve
that power and prosperity which we have seen.
But now Tiglath Pileser III (745–727) began a
new stage in Assyrian history. He restored order
to the Assyrian dominions in Mesopotamia; he
brought the province of Babylonia back into
control, eventually taking control himself under
the throne name of Pulu; he inflicted a decisive
defeat on the kingdom of Urartu; and pacified
the Medes further east. Then he set out for the
rich western lands; but this time it was not a
question of raids with tribute and booty as their
prize; the goal was conquest and assimilation
into the empire. Defeated states which refused
to submit to his suzerainty suffered not merely
reprisals but deportation.

The western states adopted the united front
which had proved successful at the Battle of
Qarqar; a coalition was formed; according to
Assyrian records, under the leadership of Uzziah,
King of Judah.[11] But this time it was of no avail
and Damascus, Israel and the others were forced

[11] Cf. *ANET*, 282.

to pay tribute. No doubt this played a part in Israel's internal dissention at this time. A crippling tax had to be imposed in order to raise the price demanded by the Assyrians (2 Kings 15.19–20), and there were some who thought it better to try once more recourse to arms. The leader of this party was Pekah, who seized the throne from Menahem's son and set about restoring the broken coalition to face Assyria. Rezon, King of Damascus, was of the same mind, and so were the Philistines. Naturally they wanted the co-operation of Judah, and when King Ahaz showed himself unwilling they declared war on him with the intention of deposing him and setting up instead one of their own supporters, Ben Tabeel. (Isa. 7.6.) At the same time the Edomites took this opportunity to regain their old territories and attacked and destroyed Ezion Geber.

Surrounded thus on all sides, Ahaz appealed to Assyria for help—stupidly, as Isaiah pointed out (Isa. 7.7–9), for Tiglath Pileser did not need this appeal nor the gift that accompanied it to be stirred into action against the revolt. He marched straight down through Israel, dealing summarily with the Philistines on the way, and established an outpost in the south to guard against any possible move from Egypt. Then he lopped off the northern limb of the rebellion,

Damascus: in 732 he destroyed the city and deported a large part of the population, so that from that moment the state ceased to have independent existence. This left only Israel to deal with. But disaster was averted by the assassination of Pekah and the unconditional surrender of the new king, Hoshea; so that Tiglath Pileser exacted only limited retribution and annexed three provinces—Dor, Megiddo and Gilead—to the empire. (Cf. Isa. 9.1.)

But Israel's madness had to run its full course. Taking advantage of the death of Tiglath Pileser, and with a vague hope of assistance from Egypt, Hoshea attempted revolt once more. This time Assyrian action was final. The country was overrun; Samaria fell in 721, after a siege of two years; large numbers of the population were deported and replaced by people who had suffered the same fate in other parts of the empire; and Israel ceased to exist.

## 3. 721–587

### 1. HEZEKIAH

The disappearance of the northern kingdom was for Judah also a disaster almost too great for comprehension. For in spite of all political differences they had continued to regard the north as still part of the same nation, and still the People of God. But for the moment they were too preoccupied with their own position to take stock of the implications of this disaster.

For throughout these tragic years Judah had not escaped unscathed. Ahaz' hasty and craven submission to Tiglath Pileser reduced the kingdom to a state of dependency on Assyria, and laid the country under a heavy financial obligation to the "deliverer". This weighed all the more heavily since it coincided with economic difficulties following on the Syro-Ephraimitic war, especially the loss of revenue from trade and industry resulting from the Edomite conquest of Ezion Geber. Ahaz had to call on the treasures of both Temple and palace to provide the necessary money, which means that taxation must already have been as high as possible.

The economic difficulties were complicated by the religious situation. Submission to Assyria involved, according to the ideas of the time, a setback for Yahweh and the victory of the gods of Assyria; and Ahaz was not so fervent a believer in Yahweh as to resist this tendency. He adopted a copy of an Assyrian altar which he saw when visiting Damascus to pay homage to Tiglath Pileser, and had it set up in the Temple; he offered his own son as a sacrifice to Moloch; and following this lead, all sorts of pagan practices went unchecked, including necromancy and idol-worship. But paganism never became so deeply rooted in Judah as it had been in the north. The danger was not so much the abandonment of the traditional faith as a distortion of it which was in a way much more dangerous and much more difficult to correct. So far from ignoring the Covenant, Judah was inclined to place too much confidence in it—as if the promise of God was something her people could rely on regardless of their own internal dispositions. (See above, p. 166.) Against all this men like Isaiah, Micah and Jeremiah had to wage a long and difficult struggle; and their preaching reveals that the public effects of this attitude were much the same in Judah as they had been in the north—injustice, dishonesty, oppression, excessive wealth battening on helpless need, abetted by corrupt judges, unreproved by venal clergy and time-serving prophets.

The shock caused by the fall of the northern kingdom, and the influence of the prophets Micah and especially Isaiah, recalled the nation to the covenant faith; and Hezekiah, who succeeded Ahaz in 715, was able to set on foot some reforms. Forms of worship incompatible with Yahwism were banned—idols and shrines where pagan gods were worshipped. He also removed from the Temple a bronze image of a serpent which was traditionally associated with a plague of serpents in Mosaic times (Num. 21.4–9), but which was capable of misinterpretation as a pagan symbol (the figure of the serpent appears frequently in Semitic iconography). A tentative effort was made to include the north in this reforming movement; with the loss of autonomy there, the political differences which had separated the kingdoms were now pointless and this seemed a suitable occasion to think of bringing the broken remnant back to the unity of the Covenant People. The overture, however, was rejected—probably because Assyrian supervision in the north was too close.

For this reform was not only a blow against Assyria's gods, but a challenge to Assyrian authority. This was made possible by Assyrian preoccupations at home. As was to be increasingly the case, the weight of empire was proving an embarrassing burden, and Assyria found itself the centre of a ring of rebellious provinces; and beyond the empire Cimmerians and Scythians were pressing in from the north. Babylon was increasingly restless, and its new leader, Merodach Baladan, was trying to organize opposition in other countries which were subject to Assyria. The final link in the chain was the new dynasty which had come to power in Egypt, under the Ethiopian Piankhi.

The simmering rebellion came prematurely to the boil in 713. The Philistine town of Ashdod refused tribute to Assyria; but other states, though tempted, did not rally to its support; Hezekiah was persuaded by Isaiah, miming the misery of captivity (ch. 20), that disaster must follow such a venture; and worst of all, Egypt, too, let them down and the Philistine town suffered alone the full weight of Assyrian vengeance.

In 705, however, Sargon II, the great conqueror of Samaria, died and was succeeded by his son Sennacherib; and at once the flame of revolt broke out throughout the west, from Tyre to Egypt. This time Hezekiah could not resist. There were secret comings and goings of envoys between Babylon and Judah and Judah and Egypt, and the warnings of Isaiah, who had not changed his views, went unheeded. Hezekiah made preparations for war, including the strengthening of the defences of Jerusalem and the construction of a tunnel to bring the water from the spring of Gihon to the pool of Siloam right inside the city walls.

But Assyria was still the greatest military power of the day. Sennacherib first subdued Babylon, not completely nor finally, but enough

to leave him free to move against the west. Tyre
was the first to fall; then he moved down the
coast and crushed the Philistine cities which had
joined the revolt. A quick victory over the
Egyptians coming to the help of their allies,
and all the other smaller states were seized with
panic and hastily offered their submission—
leaving Judah alone. One after another the
fortified cities of Judah fell to the Assyrians,
and Hezekiah was shut up in Jerusalem "like a
caged bird". From Lachish, which he then held
under siege, Sennacherib sent his general to
demand Hezekiah's surrender. The king offered
huge sums of money—which the Assyrians
accepted, but still demanded complete surrender. Hezekiah, realizing that this would mean
the end of the city and the state, determined
on resistance; and this time his policy had the
support and encouragement of Isaiah. The
prophet's conduct was not as contradictory as
it may sound; his opposition to Hezekiah's plans
in the first place had been based on the fact that
Israel should rely on God alone, not on uncertain human alliances, and now that human help
had failed he could with equal confidence preach
faith in God.

And that faith was vindicated. Some unexpected calamity suddenly struck the Assyrian

army—perhaps a plague—and brought dramatic, miraculous deliverance to Judah.[12]

This escape was sufficiently narrow to deter Hezekiah from further rashness; and the reign of his son Manasseh (686–642), coinciding with a period of strong rule in Assyria, was equally free from attempts at revolt. Sennacherib was murdered by one of his sons, but another of them, Esarhaddon, succeeded to the throne and showed himself a most capable ruler. It was under him and his successor Ashurbanipal that Egypt was finally conquered; Thebes was destroyed, and an Assyrian protégé, Neco, was installed as ruler.

## 2. THE REFORM OF JOSIAH

Manasseh was in no position to offer resistance to such power. It is true that Chronicles tells us that he was brought before his Assyrian masters in chains; but he was sent home again in favour,

[12] Cf. *ANET*, 287–8. The Assyrian records give the impression that this was a complete victory followed by the surrender of Hezekiah. This is what one would expect such records to say, but nevertheless there is some reason to think that Sennacherib actually carried out two campaigns in Judah, one in 701 as related above, ending with Hezekiah's surrender and payment of tribute, the other in 688 ending with the miraculous deliverance.

so the incident cannot be attributed to an attempted revolt, but merely to Assyria's constant suspicion of her vassal rulers. And against this is the fact that the records also tell us that Manasseh contributed to Esarhaddon's building projects, and that he even engaged in building projects of his own (2 Chron. 33.14)—which the Assyrian would scarcely have permitted if his loyalty had been suspect.

Political subservience once more was accompanied by pagan religious influence, and, as under Ahaz, this was due largely to the lead given by the king himself. The Bible draws up a long and damning indictment of the abuses which the king allowed to flourish—fertility rites, astral worship, necromancy, magic, human sacrifice, ritual prostitution; and much of this even in the Temple itself. (2 Kings 21.1–7.)

But the Yahwist religion was still strong in Judah, and when Manasseh died and his son Amon looked like continuing his father's policy, a combination of religious and political dissatisfaction led to his assassination. But no matter how much they disapproved of the current religious abuses, the propertied middle-class ("the people of the land" as the text calls them) were not prepared to face the devastation certain to result from any attempt to cast off Assyrian control; they promptly turned on the assassins and ensured the succession of Amon's son Josiah.

The most striking event of Josiah's reign—so striking that the Bible tells us practically nothing else—was the deep and far-reaching reform of religion which he carried out. To be sure, this was not a sudden and unexpected innovation due to the personal devotion of the king alone. The Yahwist faith had been weakened and corrupted by apathy, ignorance and the infiltration of foreign ideas; but the covenant faith which lay at the heart of the national being had never been repudiated or abandoned completely. In Judah it was particularly deep-rooted; partly because the population there was less diluted with Canaanite elements and less subject to the infiltration of such elements from outside (as happened to Israel at the time of Omri and Jezebel); partly because of the presence of the amphictyonic shrine as their capital, a continual reminder of their national traditions; partly because of the association of the Covenant with the dynasty of David; as we shall see, this was something of a mixed blessing, but nevertheless, just as the dynasty gained prestige and support from its association with the Covenant, so it in turn kept alive the ideal of the covenant faith. In addition, individual monarchs of Judah had been sufficiently aware of their responsibilities in this regard to take steps to maintain the purity of that faith—such had been Hezekiah, whose reforms clearly prepared the way for Josiah's far more vigorous action. And above all, the prophets had not preached in vain: Isaiah and Micah did not bring about a dramatic conversion, a nation of saints dedicated and spiritual-minded to a man, but at least they lit a flame, they held up an ideal which glowed with unprecedented fierceness, they seared men's consciences and forced them to face up, at least for a moment, to the fact of God in their lives. All of this must be borne in mind when we speak of Josiah's reform.

He first of all removed from the Temple the pagan symbols which Manasseh had permitted or introduced. The place had become little more than a pantheon, a shrine for any and every kind of deity—to a follower of Yahweh, a loathsome and horrifying spectacle. Canaanite Baal, Assyrian astral deities, sacred pillars, chariot of the sun, furnace of Moloch, the altars of the gods, "the abomination of Sidon, the abomination of Moab, the abomination of Ammon"—all of this was swept away, demolished and the rubbish scattered in the Valley of Kedron. Then the reform was extended to the rest of Judah, and then even to the north—closing down holy places where a form of worship had been practised which was either frankly idolatrous or contaminated by paganism, the priests who led this worship being put to death.

The Temple fabric had suffered from the neglect of previous years, and Josiah arranged for a complete overhaul. In the course of this an ancient book was found which, because it seemed to be of some importance, was reported to the Temple authorities and eventually brought to the notice of the king. This was the work now found as the substance of the present Deuteronomy—an edition of ancient covenant law in homiletic, hortatory style, probably composed in the northern kingdom. One may imagine that after the fall of the northern kingdom some devout Yahwist had taken refuge in the land of Judah, bringing with him this record of prophetic preaching; but the priests of Jerusalem already had their own ideas of religion, their own traditions centred round the covenant with the dynasty of David and the amphictyonic shrine of which they were the guardians; this document from the north, witness though it might be of a genuine tradition developed in difficult circumstances, could not in their eyes compare with their own traditions, and they would do no more than condescend to allow it

to take its place in the Temple archives, along
with other unneeded documents.[13]

This book, then, did not bring some completely new revelation; but it did express the
clear note of the ancient covenant faith in a form
which was not obscured by the superstition
which had clustered round the dynastic tradition. As we have seen, the danger to religion in
the south was not so much paganism, as it was in
the north, but the even more insidious distortion
of the Covenant itself. The promise to David
had come to be seen as an unconditional guarantee of permanence for the dynasty, and the
nation ruled by this line, being the people of
God's choice, were thereby inviolable. But here
in this new document the authentic note of the
primitive covenant sounded, demand as well as
promise, responsibility no less than privilege.

This uncompromising and sombre document
made a great impression on the king and court,
shocking them into a clearer realization of the
gulf between the true idea of the Covenant and
the bland complacency which had become the

[13] Cf. G. von Rad, *Studies in Deuteronomy* (1953),
with a slightly different treatment of some details; he
holds that Deuteronomy was revised as a basis for
Josiah's reform. For a fuller account of the Deuteronomic work, see again Weiser, *Introduction*, 126–35;
Robert and Feuillet, *Introduction*, vol. 1, 367–71.

norm. It has sometimes been suggested that this in fact sparked off Josiah's reform; but it seems much more likely that this had already begun (after all, the repair of the Temple, which led to the discovery of the book, implies that some steps were already being taken), but that it was given added urgency by this frightening reminder. Certainly many of the steps taken coincide with the measures advocated by Deuteronomy. This is especially true of the centralization of worship. The sad experience of the northern kingdom had shown that without strict supervision it was difficult to maintain purity of faith in the country as a whole. We have already noted that the official sanctuaries of the north, Bethel and Dan, set up for the worship of Yahweh, became associated in the minds of many with the pagan worship of the Canaanites round about, with the bull as a pagan symbol; and as Canaanite influence increased it was even easier for it to find a footing in other local sanctuaries. The same was true even in Judah. Therefore, Deuteronomy envisaged—and Josiah enforced—the extremely radical solution of forbidding any form of public worship anywhere except at Jerusalem. Local shrines had to cease functioning. Priests known to have taken part in pagan worship were put

7

to death, but now even those who had not deviated were deprived of their functions. This caused great hardship, which is reflected in the admonition of Deuteronomy that the Levite should be an object of public charity, along with the orphan, the widow and the stranger. (E.g., Deut. 14.29.) The deposed clergy were invited to Jerusalem, but this caused difficulties with those already established there, and eventually resulted in the recognition of different grades of clergy—the Jerusalem priests retained their position, and the others, who came to be known simply as "Levites", were reduced to secondary rank, with subordinate duties and privileges.

Josiah's reform was made possible by the political conditions which accompanied it. The Assyrian Empire, won by force, could only be held by force. Revolts in one part or other of their territories were a permanent feature of Assyrian rule, and the greater the empire, the greater the effort needed to sustain it, until finally it was like trying to stem a dike leaking in a dozen places at once, and the will to rule flagged and failed with the effort. Thus, a few years after the conquest of Egypt which made Assyria the greatest power the world had yet known—at least in terms of geographical control —every quarter of the empire was up in arms.

In Babylon, where the king's brother was regent, there was another bid for independence, with the help of the Elamites. Egypt and Lydia conspired together; the Medes, and behind them the Cimmerians and Scythians, were pressing in from the north. Ashurbanipal managed to deal successfully with all of this; but then, tired of the struggle, spent the rest of his reign in artistic pursuits, collecting a vast library of ancient literature to which we owe much of our knowledge of the myths and epics of the ancient world. But after Ashurbanipal's death trouble broke out again, and this time it was final. Nabopolasser was proclaimed King of Babylon and advanced up the Euphrates, while the Medes attacked from the north. In 614, Asshur fell, in 612 Nineveh, and in 610, as the Assyrians fell back further and further, Haran. The Pharao Neco chose this moment to come to the assistance of his Assyrian overlord, though more from fear of Babylon than from loyalty to Assyria. Josiah of Judah, on the other hand, who had been carrying out and extending his reforms under cover of these events, was happy to see Assyria fall and tried to bar the Pharao's route at Megiddo. He lost his life in the attempt, but the Egyptian intervention also was fruitless; and by 609 resistance in Assyria had virtually ceased.

### 3. LAST DAYS OF JUDAH

The prophet Nahum gives us a picture of the savage exultation with which the world greeted the downfall of Assyria; but in fact it merely meant the exchange of one master for another, for Babylon claimed the right of succession to the Assyrian Empire. This was what the Egyptians had feared, and they now made preparations to dispute this right, at least as far as the west was concerned. The Pharao removed Jehoahaz, son and successor of Josiah, and replaced him by his brother Eliakim (at the same time changing his name to Jehoiakim)—clear notice of his claim to Judah as a vassal state. Babylon was still engaged in consolidating its hold on the rest of the empire and did not challenge this for the moment; but when Egypt attempted to extend her claims northwards, then the clash came. In 605, the Babylonians inflicted a crushing defeat on the Egyptians at Carchemish, the following year at Hamath, and then pursued them right down to the border of Egypt itself. In the meanwhile, Nabopolassar had been succeeded by Nebuchadnezzar, and it was he who in 601 engaged the Egyptians near the frontier; but this time the Egyptians stood firm, and Nebuchadnezzar was forced to retire home to reorganize his forces. Judah then made the first of a series of fatal miscalculations; mistaking this temporary setback for the first signs of a crack in Babylonian power, they chose this moment to declare their independence. Nebuchadnezzar ordered a holding action by his dependants in the district, Arameans, Ammonites and Moabites; and then in 598 himself came with his army to settle this revolt. Jehoiakim died at this moment; and it was his son Jehoiachin who had to face the onslaught. He was taken to Babylon as a prisoner, together with other members of the court and a large number (ten thousand, according to Kings) of important citizens. In his place the Babylonians appointed his uncle under the name of Zedekiah.

But now confusion returned to Judah, a "spirit of drunkenness and reeling" as the prophets would say. Josiah's reform had lapsed in the confusion of the past few years, and the old "covenant superstition" had returned. This superstition attached particularly to Jerusalem, the city where God himself had his dwelling-place and which was thereby considered inviolable; the miraculous deliverance of the city in 701 had fostered this idea, and even the reform of Josiah, with its centralization of cult, had the unintended effect of increasing the prestige of this unique sanctuary and encouraging superstitious trust in its efficacy as a talisman. Even the law of God, on which the reform was based, had been distorted and emptied of real meaning, and equated with the magic incantations of pagan rituals; one need only perform the prescribed gestures and the desired result would be achieved, regardless of personal dispositions. This is what gives such anguish to the preaching of Jeremiah at this time; for he saw that in these circumstances, there was no hope for any further reform; for what guarantee was there that the same distortion would not be practised on any other formula for national renewal? He foresees instead a remedy more drastic than any hitherto envisaged; nothing less than destruction. In the existing mood of the nation, nothing less than amputation reaching to the heart would do. And in that mood, the people was prepared to risk a folly so great that it would in fact bring about the remedy Jeremiah saw.

Zedekiah was in a difficult position; for with Jehoiachin alive though captive in Babylon, he was held by the majority of the people to have only a doubtful title to authority, and at best as no more than regent. This insecurity, coupled with his own indecisive character, foretells the course of his political policy or lack of one, swinging from one extreme to another as he comes under the influence of one or other party. One school of thought was in favour of pacifism, of accepting the dominion of Babylon and making the best of it until better times should come. Others were fiercely nationalist, eager to embark on a war of independence; Babylon was indeed powerful, but they could form a united front with other states in the same position as themselves, especially Egypt.

Eventually, with Egyptian instigation, the nationalists prevailed, and rebellion broke out —for the last time. The Babylonians reacted promptly. One army swiftly surrounded Jerusalem, while another concentrated on taking the other fortified towns in Judah. The last of these to fall was Lachish, and letters found in the ashes of the city betray the despair of the garrison before its inevitable doom.[14] Finally Jerusalem alone remained. For a moment the siege was raised while the Babylonians went out to deal with an Egyptian army advancing to the help of their ally, and for a moment hope surged and men began to recall the deliverance from Sennacherib. But Jeremiah continued his preaching of the certainty of disaster, and in 587 his words were proved true. The city fell. Zedekiah was caught as he attempted to flee, his two sons were slaughtered before his eyes and then

[14] Cf. *ANET*, 322.

his eyes were put out, and he was taken off in chains. With him went a further batch of the population. The city was burnt to the ground, and its walls were demolished. Judah had ceased to exist.

One further spasm of insanity set the final seal on this humiliation. The Babylonians incorporated the territory of Judah into their empire, as a province under its own governor, Gedaliah. He was assassinated by a group of fanatics; and in revenge, the Babylonians wiped out even the name and province of Judah, uniting it with the neighbouring province of Samaria.

# THE NEW COMMUNITY

LITTLE is known in detail of the conditions of life in exile—the Bible is silent on this bitter period of Israel's history—but a little more can be gathered by inference.

## 1. DISASTER AND RECOVERY

Material conditions were not as difficult as they might have been. There was some restriction on liberty, of course; but the people were allowed to settle in self-contained communities, to earn their own living, and even, if they wished, to take part in the social life and commerce of the Babylonians.

But spiritually the spark of national life was never nearer to extinction than during this period. For here was a people whose existence rested on a faith, and that faith had fallen. They existed as a people, they held, in virtue of Yahweh's choice—Yahweh, the God who was faithful and true, whose promise to them could not and would not fail; this was the faith which had led them from Sinai, and it had persisted, though with deviations and distortion, right up to the very eve of the disaster. Now, then, a dilemma faced them: Either this God was no God at all, or if he were all they thought, then he had finally cast them off. Either way lay despair.

And everything in their present circumstances was calculated to increase that despair. This was the first time that they had come into direct contact with a civilization other than their own, and the experience brought about a complete upheaval in their ideas. They had of course known the armies of Assyria and Babylon, ambassadors from Egypt, traders from far-off countries; but now they were brought face to face with a wealth and power they had never dreamed of. They gazed in astonishment at the wide streets and flowing canals, the bustle of people and shops selling wares from every quarter of the world, the magnificent buildings, the great Processional Way from the Ishtar Gate to the *ziggurat* of Marduk, the colossal statues which seemed to symbolize the power of Babylon—and of her gods. How could they have ever been so naïve as to think that Jerusalem was anything other than a petty provincial capital? How could they have thought that Yahweh could prevail against such might?

Undoubtedly there were many who succumbed to the pressure to conform and were assimilated into the heterogeneous flotsam of nations in Babylon at the time. But the astonishing thing is that anything at all survived the wreck, and that the national identity was not completely lost. That this did not happen may be attributed to the teaching of the Prophets, three in particular: Jeremiah, whose work spans the disaster of 587, though he himself was not among the exiles (after the murder of Gedaliah he was taken to Egypt, against his will, by a group fleeing Babylonian reprisals); Ezekiel, a man of priestly family who preached from one of the settlements near Babylon; and an anonymous prophet whose work is found in Isaiah 40–55.

These men, each in his own way, provided an explanation of the disaster which at the same time formed a foundation for the building of faith anew. At the very moment when Israel was crushed with the sense of her own insignificance, these men reached out exultantly to the thought of the immensity of their God: God of all time, of all lands, of all peoples. And all history and all peoples are servants of his will. That Babylon was triumphant and Israel crushed beneath its heel, this was not a sign of the impotence of their God, but precisely the proof of his power. Nor did it put in doubt their faith that they had been God's Chosen People, but confirmed it; for they were chosen to be his servants, and they had failed; such a God demands total service, and they had honoured him with their lips while their hearts were far from him. Considering the sins of Israel and the holiness of Israel's God, then their downfall was not an incomprehensible disaster—it was inevitable. But, the prophets now went on to say, this did not mean that God had cast off his people finally. This disaster was not the vengeance of an outraged God tried beyond endurance. Its purpose was not destruction, but healing. It was the fate, but it was also the privilege, of the exiles to bear the burden of the previous years of infidelity, and by bearing it to atone for it.[1] Out of this furnace of suffering a new and purified remnant would return, small in number but great with the honour of bearing God's glory to the world, of being a light to the Gentiles.

So, precisely on the ruins of the old, the prophets laid the foundations of a new faith. The next step was to build a way of life which would express and sustain this new faith, now that there were no Temple, sacrifice, magnificent liturgy and joyful feasts. But these things had

[1] For a full discussion of the interpretation of the "Suffering Servant" passages on which this is based, see C. R. North, *The Suffering Servant in Deutero-Isaiah*, 2nd ed. (1956).

been one of the main elements in the previous distortion of religion—these ceremonial practices fulfilled, all obligation to God was thought to be fulfilled. To replace these now there was only something much deeper and much simpler—the word of God; the fact that God had spoken to Israel, had chosen them, had made a covenant with them. This word of God was expressed in their history; and these national traditions were now carefully collected and treasured as the very substance of their faith.

There were the words of the prophets whose harsh message had so often met with derision during their lifetime but which was now proved by the event. Then there was the copy of the Law found in the Temple during the reign of Josiah, from which the later Book of Deuteronomy developed; how poignantly its challenge sounded now: "Behold I set before you this day life and good, death and evil. If you obey the commandments of the Lord your God, you shall live. But if your heart turns away, I declare to you this day that you shall perish; you shall not live long in the land . . ." (Cf. Deut. 30.15–18.) It was in the same spirit, too, that the earlier traditions were now viewed, those dealing with the period from Israel's entry into Canaan right down to the time of the destruction of Jerusalem —the work which the Hebrew Bible calls "the former prophets", Joshua to Kings. Then there were the even earlier traditions already embodied in the work of J and E, now fused into one.

But the composition of J and E had not put a stop to oral tradition, and another form of these traditions was preserved, especially by the priests, and is known therefore as P.[2] The priestly traditions concerning the worship practised in the Temple were also put on record against the day when it could once more be carried out in its ancient splendour. And with these two were linked other regulations expressive of the priestly concern for legal correctness in religious matters. This was not simply a matter of narrow formalism; devotion was primarily a matter of the heart, but it was important that it should be given concrete expression; and especially at that time, when it was urgently necessary to preserve a sense of identity in the lost and wandering group of exiles, to prevent them being swamped in the mass of peoples,

[2] Cf. Weiser, *Introduction*, 135–42; Robert and Feuillet, *Introduction*, vol. 1, 372–80. It is not suggested that the whole of the Bible, or even the whole of the Pentateuch, was completed at this time; this was not done till some time after the exile, probably in the period after Ezra and before the Seleucids. But the process must have begun now, during the Exile. Cf. H. H. Rowley, *The Growth of the Old Testament* (1950).

it is not surprising that there should be a certain stress on such customs as differentiated them from the rest—Sabbath, circumcision and ritual cleanliness. In the circumstances of the time (whatever may become true later), zeal for the Law was the sign of personal acceptance of the Covenant. It was the expression of that personal responsibility which the prophets of this period preached. Previously it had been too easy to shrug off individual guilt onto the more impersonal corporate body, and the prophets strove to drive home the idea that the community was nothing without the individuals which composed it, and that each individual must bear responsibility for his own acts: "No longer shall this be a proverb amongst you: 'The fathers have eaten sour grapes and the children's teeth have been set on edge'; but the soul that sins, the same shall die." (Ezek. 18.1–4; Jer. 31.29–30.)

Undoubtedly the influence of the priests was strong at this time; but the situation was too serious for any narrow partisanship, and representatives of both the priestly and the prophetic spirit were among the new leaders who now emerged to do this work of collecting and preserving and teaching the word of God—these new "servants of the word" who were to be known as "scribes". In any case, it would be wrong to make too great an antithesis between the priestly and the prophetic spirit. It is true that the prophets stressed above all the personal and internal aspect of religion while the priests were the custodians of its institutional forms; but no matter how critical the prophets were of the dead letter of the law, of a formalism which claimed to be the essence of religion, there was never any question of their disavowing the institution.[3]

The Judean exiles, then, did survive and did maintain their identity. Slowly and painfully they picked themselves up and began to repair the wreck of their lives. They "built themselves houses and planted gardens", as Jeremiah recommended them. (Jer. 29.5.) They found employment in their old trades—there was a high proportion of craftsmen amongst the men deported (2 Kings 24.14)—and even in the Babylonian government administration. But they also met together on the Sabbath day in the "house of assembly", the synagogue, for a service in which the essential element was the reading of the sacred writings. They did not forget their

[3] On the connection between the prophets and official religion, see H. H. Rowley, *The Unity of the Bible* (1953), 30–48. The close relationship between priest and prophet is exemplified in the person of Ezekiel, who is both priest and prophet, and whose prophetic work embodies many themes characteristic of the priestly tradition.

past; Babylon was always an alien land from which they turned their eyes longingly to their real home and Jerusalem its capital:

> By the waters of Babylon we sat and wept,
> Remembering Zion.
> On the willows there we hung up our harps.
> Our captors there asked us a song,
> Our conquerors asked us to rejoice:
> "Sing us one of the songs of Zion."
>
> How shall we sing the song of the Lord
> In an alien land?
> If I forget thee, Jerusalem, let my right hand wither;
> Let my tongue be fixed in my mouth if I remember not thee.          (Ps. 137.1–6.)

So, after the first blackness of despair, hope returned to the exiles, and for fifty years they lived on that hope. Then political events began to give some substance to their hopes, and the exiles watched with anxiety and excitement the career of one who almost seemed to be sent by God to be their deliverer. (Isa. 45.1–6:48.12–15.)

The kingdom of Media, east of Babylon, had been first Babylon's ally in the struggle against Assyria, and later her rival for world power. But in 550, a subject king of the Medes, Cyrus of Persia, rebelled against his overlord and made himself master of the Median Empire. By 546 he was in a position to challenge Croesus of Lydia, the greatest power to the west; in a surprise attack he captured the capital Sardis, and brought Lydia under his control.

The next objective, it was obvious to everyone, was the Empire of Babylon itself. The Babylonians on their part give the impression of awaiting their fate with indifference and resignation—it is almost as if they had struggled so long for independence that they were exhausted by the effort. The king, Nabonidus, had retired to Teima in Arabia, leaving his son Belshazzar in charge of the government. By 539 Cyrus was ready to attack—and Babylon was ready to succumb. There was one battle—at Opis on the Tigris—and then Babylon surrendered without a struggle.

Cyrus was not an oriental tyrant such as the world had known up to that time. The normal policy of conquerors previous to this had been slaughter, destruction, deportation, slavery and savage repression. But the conduct of Cyrus as victor was characterized by clemency; this was partly due to his own temperament, but partly also for political motives—he was aware that an immense slave population was a potential source of danger to the state, as had been shown in his own campaign against Babylon. One of his earliest measures as ruler, then, was the restoration of political and religious freedom to the subject peoples of the empire he had inherited.

## 2. THE RETURN FROM EXILE

Among those who benefited by the new policy were the exiles from Judah, and preparations were immediately made to take advantage of it. But in spite of the grief they had felt at the loss of their land, and in spite of the devotion to the Holy City which had been nurtured in exile, there was no mass movement to return. The exile had lasted a full generation; many had little recollection of any other life than that of Babylon; many had formed ties and attachments which could not be broken at once; many preferred to wait and allow others to prepare the way for them. It was therefore a fairly small party of the more adventurous or ardent spirits who gathered together a few possessions and set out on the long journey back to the Promised Land.

During the weary years of waiting one of the prophets had bolstered up their faith with the thrilling prospect of a new Exodus, a new manifestation of God's power and his care for his own, leading them from captivity to freedom. (Isa. 40.) But when this first party actually arrived in their land, the conditions they found there were enough to dismay the boldest. The land still bore the marks of the destruction wrought by the Babylonian conquerors; the Holy City was still in ruins, the land was a wilderness, and wherever it could still provide a livelihood it had been taken over by the Edomites.

In these sorry conditions the returned exiles settled down as best they could. It is a tribute to the faith which motivated them that their first care was the restoration of worship. An altar was set up in the ruins of the holy place, and a beginning was made on the rebuilding of the Temple itself. But under the burden of misery and despair the work stumbled to a halt.

In the next few years other caravans arrived from Babylon, notably one led by a member of the royal family, Zerubbabel, with the priest Joshua as his right-hand man. The spirits of the small community improved a little with this increase in their numbers; but it was above all the appearance of two prophets, Haggai and Zechariah, which stirred the people to life again. Under the encouragement and reproaches of these two, the rebuilding of the Temple was resumed, and this time it was brought to a successful conclusion. Successful, that is, in that the building was at least completed. But there were many who saw in the contrast between Solomon's magnificent structure and the modest building which was all that could be achieved now a symbol of the sad decline of their fortunes.

But it was a symbol also of at least survival. At least the Temple was there, where previously there had been only a heap of ruins. And the people were once more in their land. The exact political position of the new community is uncertain. Sheshbazzar, the leader of the first party to return, is called "governor"; but this is a vague term, and it seems probable that the territory alloted to them came under the control of the governor of the Persian province of Samaria, with the Jewish national leaders acting as something like high commissioners for Jewish affairs within the province.

The temporary stimulus to the national spirit which led to the completion of the Temple coincided with a stirring period in the Persian Empire as a whole. The death of Cyrus's successor Cambyses in 522 BC was taken as the signal for a general upheaval; everywhere provinces were in revolt, and for a time it looked as if the empire might crumble. This encouraged even higher hopes in Judah, and the prophets even spoke of Zerubbabel in messianic terms. (Zech. 3.9:6.10–13.)

These hopes did not last; Darius I was an energetic and capable ruler who subdued the revolts and established himself firmly in

authority. But the ferment caused by these
troubles did contribute to increasing Judah's
difficulties with the Samaritans. From the very
first, economic and religious difficulties had
resulted in strained relations between the two
peoples. The religious difficulties stemmed from
the peculiar position of the Samaritans resulting
from their history. When the northern tribes
were all but wiped out by the Assyrians, their
place was filled by other deported peoples. These
conformed to the religious customs of their new
home, but naturally with no very clear understanding or careful observance. (2 Kings 17.24–
41.) Nevertheless, they still claimed to share the
same religious traditions as their southern neighbours, and when they saw the sorry band of exiles
returning to Judah they hoped that their misery
would make them forget the trifling differences
between them. But the returned exiles were not
more broadminded than before, but even less
inclined than ever to disregard religious differences. They were convinced that they alone
were the true remnant of Israel in whom the real
heart of the nation lived on; they had little
enough regard for their kinsmen who had remained in Judah, and they were still less ready
to recognize or accept friendly gestures from the
Samaritans. From an economic point of view, the
Samaritans had remained in possession of their

land and in relative prosperity while the exiles were enduring the hardships of captivity and the misery of the return; while the Samaritans on their part, after an initial rebuff by the Jews,[4] did not welcome the prospect of a strong Jewish state on their borders and perhaps ultimately a challenge to their own security. They did all in their power, then, to hinder the Jewish revival, and in particular they tried to stir up trouble for them with the Persian authorities, hoping that Darius would see in the rebuilding of the Temple a suspicion of impending rebellion like those with which he had to contend on assuming power. In this, however, the Samaritans were unsuccessful; Darius instead confirmed the Jewish rights, leaving the Samaritans to plot other ways of dealing with the situation.

The building of the Temple, then, was completed; and with this, the Jewish return was an established fact. They had struck roots. But it was by no means a strong and thriving plantation, and the continued existence of the community was by no means assured. In this state they struggled on for another fifty years, never

[4] Israel, the people of the twelve tribes, no longer existed. Ten of those tribes, which had made up the northern kingdom overrun by the Assyrians, had disappeared. All that remained was the remnant of the southern kingdom, Judah. This is why the people from this time are known as the Judeans, the Jews.

completely certain from year to year that their little community could survive; until, from Babylon again, two other leaders came whose enthusiasm and faith made the future finally assured.

### 3. NEHEMIAH AND EZRA

Nehemiah held an official position at the Persian court, but he followed the history of his fellow Jews in Judah with the keenest interest and with sympathy for their hard lot. Finally, disturbed by the news brought back by visitors from Jerusalem, he requested permission from his master, Artaxerxes I, to go there himself. The king granted permission, and even gave him the rank of Governor of Judah as a province separate from Samaria.

Nehemiah made material reconstruction his first task. A Temple had indeed been built, and the people had made homes of a sort for themselves; but the Holy City was still virtually in the same condition in which the Babylonians had left it. It was Nehemiah's dream to see this city restored, if not to its former glory, at least to some semblance of order, with its own walls rising proudly around it. Immediately after his arrival, then, he spent some time secretly surveying the site, noting the needs and the difficulties and making plans for the work of rebuilding. Then he called a council of the leaders on the spot, announced his appointment and royal commission, and gave orders for work to be started at once. There was little difficulty with materials; his mandate from the king included the right to draw on the royal parks for timber. The labour force was provided by the people as a whole, divided into groups each responsible for a set portion of the work. And in fifty-two days, according to Nehemiah 6.15, a wall was built; little more than a façade no doubt, and leaving much to be completed and strengthened later; but nevertheless a clear testimony to the energy and determination and driving power of the new governor, and a token of Judah's will to survive.

This determination was very necessary, for the surrounding peoples found their fears confirmed by this new wind in Judah and renewed their efforts to bring it to a halt. Sanballat, Governor of Samaria, Tobiah, Governor of Ammon, and Geshem, Governor of the Province of Arabia, joined forces to stop Nehemiah. They could do nothing directly against one who had the king's authority just as much as they had, but they could and did use all kinds of indirect methods. They encouraged armed bands to raid the territory—so that the builders had to work

continually under the protection of an armed
guard. They threatened to accuse Nehemiah to
the king of treason and attempted secession.
They tried to entice him to a discussion outside
Jerusalem, where they could put him to death.
And in addition to these external difficulties he
had to fight against the apathy and laxity of the
Jews themselves. Many had come to terms with
the condition of life as it was, and while this
was not particularly noble from either a material
or a spiritual point of view, it was comfortable
enough and much less demanding than the
idealism of Nehemiah.

But at the same time as Nehemiah was concen-
trating on the material restoration, Ezra arrived
to undertake the work of moral reform.[5] Like
Nehemiah, he too was armed with the king's
commission, this time for the reorganization of

[5] According to the Bible, Ezra came to Jerusalem in
the seventh year of Artaxerxes (Ezra 7.7), while Nehemiah came in the twentieth year (Neh. 2.1). But the
whole relationship of the two men seems to indicate
that Nehemiah arrived first; when Ezra arrived the wall
was already built (Ezra 9.9); he read the Law in the
presence of the whole people and of Nehemiah (Neh.
8.1–9); etc. Therefore it is suggested that the Artaxerxes
referred to in the case of Ezra is Artaxerxes II; this
would make Nehemiah's arrival 445 and Ezra's 398.
Others again consider this too late, and so amend the
phrase "seventh year" to "thirty-seventh year", thus
giving the date of Ezra's arrival as 428.

the legal administration: in practice, this meant establishing the Jewish law as the law of state with royal backing.

What exactly this law was which Ezra was empowered to enforce is uncertain, but it was most probably some form of our present Pentateuch. In other words, although as far as the Persian authorities were concerned this was merely another example of their general policy of administering their provinces according to local custom, as far as Judah was concerned this was to be a religious as well as an administrative reform. Indeed, in addition to his commission as "scribe of the Law", Ezra brought with him subsidies for the Temple itself and permission to draw on the official treasury of the province for further sums. He was empowered to appoint judges and to see that the Law was properly understood by the whole population.

Ezra began his work with a solemn reading of the Law, and then proceeded to bring practice into line with it. It is evident that in the struggle for mere existence standards had deteriorated sadly. Nehemiah had already had to deal with an old evil of pre-exilic days—even in their common distress there were profiteers ready to take advantage of the greater misfortune of others, providing loans on conditions which were equivalent to slavery. Nehemiah was disgusted and exasperated at this, and took the lead in sharing freely anything he possessed with those in need. And if this were the situation where common charity was concerned, it was to be expected that the minutiae of legal observance would fare even worse. Here the priests, whose responsibility this was, were the main offenders. Malachi lets us see how quickly—soon after the rebuilding of the Temple—abuses appeared in the way they were carrying out their duties: carelessness about the quality of the sacrifices, excessive care about payment for their own services. The same spirit of venality no doubt accounts for their collaboration with the powerful Tobiah, Governor of Ammon: as his name indicates, he claimed to be a worshipper of Yahweh, but his orthodoxy was open to suspicion—certainly Nehemiah would have nothing to do with him; yet the priestly authorities set aside a room for his use in the very Temple precincts. Similarly, marriages were contracted between priestly families and members of that other enemy of the Jewish state, the family of Sanballat, Governor of Samaria.

Ezra, with Nehemiah's active support, took vigorous action against all such breaches of the law of God. An annual tax was arranged for the upkeep of the services of the Temple, thus freeing the clergy from undue care for their livelihood and permitting them to concentrate more singlemindedly on the proper performance of their duties. Sabbath observance was more strictly enforced. And above all, mixed marriages, especially among the clergy, were dissolved.

It says much for the zeal and devotion of Ezra that he managed to engage the willing co-operation of, first, the leading members of the community, and then through them, of the people as a whole, in carrying through these reforms. Some of them, such as the dismissal of foreign wives, must have entailed real hardship; and all of them entailed some discomfort in a community which had grown accustomed to a laxer way of life.

But when the work was finished, and the whole nation gathered together for a solemn renewal of the Covenant, Ezra and Nehemiah could claim the privilege of being the new founders of the nation, now for the first time since the Exile secure, God's people living in God's land according to the law of God.

# THE END OF THE BEGINNING

## 1. THE CLOISTER AND THE WORLD

THE reformed state of Judah was in some ways more like a religious community than a political organization. The days of political greatness were over, the days when Israel counted for something in the world; and the new community turned instead to religious pursuits. There was no king now; the Temple, not the palace, was the centre of the national life; and in place of government officials concerned with the administration of the state, the books of Chronicles and Ezra devote significant space to a minute account of the various grades of clergy with their rights and responsibilities. This now was their life; not wars, treaties, economic affairs and diplomatic manoeuvres, but liturgy and religious affairs. The wall which Nehemiah had laboured to raise up round Jerusalem was symbolic; as a defence against military attack its value must have been slight, but it was a bulwark against the encroachment of foreign influences, a bulwark such as Ezra had tried to provide internally by his labours for the Law. Behind this double barrier, the People of God were to devote themselves to their first duty, the service of God, shut off from all distracting contact with the world outside.

In the world outside meanwhile great events were taking place. The Persian Empire began to expand outwards, and came into contact with the Greek states. At first, the immense superiority of Persian arms and the divided interests of the Greek states made Persian victory seem inevitable. But the empire was already too large, and internal dissensions and revolts helped the Greeks in their determined defence of their freedom.

While the Great King was patching up affairs inside his empire and preparing to launch another attack, the Greek states—although unwillingly—found another champion, Philip of Macedon. He imposed a degree of unity on the independent Greek democracies which enabled them to resist the Persians; and his son Alexander reversed the tide of conquest, crossed into Asia, and swept the Persian forces before him. After a brief detour through Palestine down to Egypt to protect his flank, Alexander continued his advances right across the Persian Empire and into India. Master of the world at the age of thirty-three, he died in Babylon in 323 BC.

There was no single obvious successor to Alexander, and after his death the empire was torn by intrigue and fighting between rival claimants, at the end of which the eastern part of the empire was shared between two generals, Ptolemy in Egypt and Seleucus in Asia. Palestine lay between the two, but by 300 BC Ptolemy had succeeded in incorporating it into his share of the empire.

Through all these eventful years, the state of Judah remained unmoved; the wall remained intact. The Jews must have heard of Marathon, Thermopylae, and Salamis; they must have seen the armies of Alexander marching past and the Persian garrisons withdrawing; they must have suffered hardship in the struggle for power which followed Alexander's death. But as long as these changes left their own position unaltered, they were content to let them pass by. And their position remained unchanged. Under the Persians they had achieved the position of an independent province within the empire, with their own law and their own government; and there is no reason to think that succeeding rulers would find it necessary to change this position. Certainly there is evidence that the Ptolemies did not interfere with the status of other provinces which they took over from the Persians; among the correspondence of the finance department

of one of the Ptolemies two letters have been discovered from Tobiah of Ammon—a descendant
of the Tobiah mentioned in the Book of Ezra
as holder of the same position, Governor of
Ammon. We know also that Judah was permitted to mint its own coinage—coins dating
from the fourth century have been found bearing the inscription *Yehud* (Judah).

But no matter how unmoved Judah may have
appeared, there was a spirit abroad in those
years which could not be ignored. The conquests of Alexander did not mean merely one
more change of power like the many which
Israel had already experienced in the course of
her long history. This was a new thing in history
—the meeting of east and west. Not that the two
had been completely isolated and cut off from
each other before this time[1]; but now for the
first time they were united in one empire; and
it was Alexander's intention that they should
form in fact one world. His soldiers were encouraged to marry and settle down on foreign
soil, forming little Greek colonies from the Indus
to the Mediterranean. Greek became the common means of communication between all parts

---

[1] Cf. C. H. Gordon, *Before the Bible* (1962), which
tries to make out a stronger case on this subject than
yet seems possible, but still gives much useful and
interesting information.

8

of the vast empire—though, as with English today, it would undergo certain changes in the process. Greek ways of life and thought stirred the old world to new life and vigour.

It was hardly possible for the Jews to be unaffected by this new spirit; such influences cannot be barred by walls. In any case, the majority of the Jews were now outside the walls of Jerusalem. Not all the exiles of Babylon had taken advantage of the Persian decree of liberation to return to Palestine; many had already settled down in Babylon and found success and prosperity there which it was difficut to exchange for the hazards and hardships of life in Palestine. For every one like Nehemiah, who broke off a successful career to help affairs in Judah, there must have been hundreds like the Jewish banking family of Murashu and Sons, whose records from the fifth century have come down to us. Others again, at various times in those difficult 200 years from the fall of Jerusalem, had emigrated voluntarily and set up Jewish communities in Asia Minor, in Greece and above all in Egypt.

About one such community we are relatively well informed, and what we learn of this one enables us to form some idea of what happened elsewhere. This community existed at Elephantine, on the Upper Nile—how, why or when it was established is unknown; possibly it was started by people who took refuge there when the Babylonians destroyed Jerusalem (like those mentioned in Jer. 43.1–7); possibly by exiles who left Babylon when the Persians gave them freedom but who could not face the rigours of life in Palestine. The Persians found the community already in existence when they annexed Egypt in 525, and in accordance with general Persian policy confirmed their right to follow their own customs. But this privilege, plus the fact that these customs included the sacrifice of animals sacred to the Egyptians, roused the hostility of their Egyptian neighbours, and during a riot in 410 their temple was burned down. The efforts to rebuild this temple resulted in the correspondence from which our information comes. The Jews of Elephantine wrote to the high priest in Jerusalem, to the Governor of Judah and to the Samaritan authorities, in an attempt to engage their interest in the work of rebuilding. Several interesting facts emerge from this correspondence. In the first place, we note the peculiarities in the form of worship practised at Elephantine; not only did they feel no hesitation in having a temple with sacrifices (contrary to the legislation of Deuteronomy); but in this temple several divinities were worshipped— possibly all representing merely different aspects of the one God, but we may doubt whether the worshippers were very clear about it. We notice also the ambiguous nature of the links between the Jews at Elephantine and those in Palestine. Clearly, Palestine was still regarded as the mother-country, even by these Jews who had probably never seen it, having been born and brought up in Egypt. On the other hand, these Jews in far-off places were not very clear about the exact position there—they wrote to both Jerusalem and Samaria, apparently unaware of the breach between them. The authorities in Jerusalem did not reply to this letter; the kind of worship which the letters bear witness to would hardly meet with the approval of the authorities there in the atmosphere of growing rigorism which had already rebuffed the Samaritans.

We may presume that other emigrants too continued to look to Jerusalem as their spiritual home. But these would be much more open to the foreign influences with which they were in such close contact. Already, since the return from exile, Hebrew had become a strange tongue to the majority of the people, and in the synagogue services it had become customary to follow the reading of the Law in Hebrew by an Aramaic paraphrase, called a *targum*. Among the Greek-speaking communities, the same necessity now led to the use of Greek translations, and by the third century a complete translation of the Pentateuch—the Septuagint—had been made.

Even in Palestine itself the influence of Hellenism was felt: Greek colonies grew up on the sites of ancient cities—Sebaste (Samaria), Philadelphia (Amman), Scythopolis (Beth Shan); and in these towns the people of Judah would have first-hand experience of Greek language, Greek buildings, Greek customs.

Judah was not so quickly won over to the new ways (although it is noticeable that the coins referred to above were in the shape of an Attic drachma, with an image of the owl of Athena on one side); but the main influence of Hellenism is to be seen in a readiness to give new thought to accepted ideas. The Book of Job, for example, brings into confrontation two schools of thought in regard to the problem of suffering. On the one hand were the representatives of the traditional view, that suffering was always the result of sin; and no matter what difficulties this view may cause, to doubt or deny it would be to bring into question the divine justice. Against this, the author presents the anguished protest of Job, that this smug and facile dogmatism offers no solace at all to one who has actual experience of the problem. The author himself does not seem to have a solution; but what is significant is his refusal to accept the traditional opinion. Less violently, but even more agnostically, the conventional view is also questioned by Qoheleth: "Vanity of vanities, and all is vanity."[2] And Jonah satirizes the narrow exclusive nationalism which would put all pagans irrevocably beyond the reach of divine mercy.

This period, then, externally so barren of historical event, was internally a time of ferment and questioning. It was a period not unlike that of the founding of the monarchy, or of the Exile. It was a period such as must occur in the history of any society which is not to fossilize and cease to have any meaning. Accepted ideas, traditional institutions and practices must be re-examined in the light of contemporary ideas, so as to distinguish between what is essential and what can be, and perhaps must be, discarded as no longer relevant. And as might be expected in such circumstances, two opposing parties emerged: there were those whose inherent conservatism reacted strongly against any suggestion of change —what had been handed down from their fathers was sacred, to tamper with it was to undermine the foundations of their national way of life and their faith; and there were those

[2] For further reading on the post-exilic literature generally, one may consult T. Henshaw, *The Writings* (1963).

whose spirits were crushed by the dead weight of 2000 years of tradition and who thrilled with the excitement of the new ideas and drew from them new hope, new vigour.

This is a temperamental rather than a dogmatic division; the conservatives could admit that not everything new was therefore false; and the "modernists" had no intention of discarding their ancestral faith; only, they would say, we must be prepared to move with the times; in ideas and customs which are an inheritance from such a distant past, there is bound to be much which is meaningless today and which we should be prepared to discard in favour of forms more in keeping with the spirit of our age. On both sides there would be exaggerations; but the positions were not irreconcilable and a solution could have been found, as it was in the days of the monarchy; but before such a solution had been worked out, a crisis was precipitated through political events.

## 2. The Struggle for Independence

The Seleucids had never accepted the Ptolemies' occupation of Palestine and Phoenicia, and about the beginning of the second century Antiochus III felt strong enough to challenge their claims. At the battle of Paneas in 198, the Seleucids were victorious and took possession of these territories which they considered their own. But this was only one move in a general policy of expansion which brought Antiochus into conflict with Rome. He gave asylum to Rome's defeated enemy Hannibal, and advanced into Greece. The Roman reaction was unhesitating and decisive; Antiochus was defeated in battle and forced to accept humiliating peace terms, which included not only the payment of a large sum of money but also the surrender of his own son as a hostage.

On the death of Antiochus III in 175, this son returned home to rule as Antiochus IV Epiphanes. Under his rule, relationships with the Jews rapidly deteriorated. The Jews had welcomed Antiochus III, and he on his side had recognized the privileged position of this small community. But this now changed. Antiochus IV shared his father's ambition to be a new Alexander, and saw in a single Hellenistic culture a powerful unifying influence for his empire. His ambitions, however, were costly, and this, together with the heavy financial burden laid on him by Rome, led the king to take desperate measures in his search for money. More than once he plundered sanctuaries within his empire; and it was inevitable that he should cast covetous eyes on Jerusalem.

There was already a pro-Hellenist party in Jerusalem; and many of its strongest supporters were members of the priestly class. One of these, who had adopted the Greek name of Jason, was ambitious for the office of high priest, and offered the king money and support for his policy of Hellenization in return for the position. The king agreed; Jason became high priest, and kept his side of the bargain. Greek customs received official encouragement, and above all the most typical of Greek institutions, a gymnasium, was introduced into Jerusalem. This caused great resentment among the traditionalists, not only because it outraged Jewish ideas of propriety, but also because of the connection between the games and pagan religious festivals. But a few years later, another aspirant to office, Menelaus, out-bid Jason, and once more the king intervened and removed Jason to make way for Menelaus. In 169, while the king was campaigning in Egypt, a rumour started that he was dead; and Jason took advantage of this to try to regain his position by force. But the rumour was false, and the king restored Menelaus and used the incident as a pretext to loot the Temple.

These events were sufficient to make it clear to the Jews that the period of coexistence with the occupying power was over. But there was worse to come. While this sordid story was taking place in Jerusalem, Antiochus had continued with his plans for expansion. In 169 he waged a successful campaign in Egypt—this was the occasion for the rumour of his death which tempted Jason to attempt to regain authority. But the following year, 168, Antiochus descended on the Egyptians again, only to find that in the meanwhile the Romans had taken the Egyptians under their protection, and was forced to withdraw in disgrace. Smarting under this humiliation, Antiochus was in no mood to tolerate any further opposition to his will from peoples under his control. He commanded that the privileged position of the Jews was to cease, and that they should be obliged, by force if necessary, to follow the same way of life as was the rule for the rest of the empire. A Hellenistic enclave, with a citadel and garrison—the Acra— was set up in Jerusalem itself. Jewish customs, such as circumcision and the prohibition of certain foods, were forbidden. The sacred books were banned and all copies found were burned. Altars were set up where the Jews were forced to sacrifice to the pagan gods. In the Temple itself an altar to Zeus was erected—the "abomination of desolation" referred to in Daniel.

This phrase expresses the horror which the vast majority of the Jews felt when faced with these new demands of Antiochus. No matter how pro-Greek many of them may have been, only a handful of renegades could accept these violations of their deepest beliefs. The Book of Daniel is one form which the reaction took—a cryptic account of these terrible days, described under the figures of the Babylonian King Nebuchadnezzar and the faithful Israelite Daniel, showing the certain downfall of the pagan oppressor and the ultimate triumph of the kingdom of the saints. Another form of reaction is seen in the conduct of a group of traditionalists known as the "Hasidim"—"the pious ones"—who either suffered death in passive resistance or took refuge in the hills beyond the reach of the king's officials.

But there were some who felt that resistance should not be limited to pacifism or to purely literary weapons. To these the lead was given by Mattathias and his five sons, whose deeds are recorded in the two books of Maccabees.[3] When

[3] The works known as 1 and 2 Maccabees are two quite different books; the first is written in Hebrew in the style of the ancient biblical histories, the second is Greek both in language and style, full of rather rhetorical appeals to the reader's emotions. The only reason for linking them together is their common subject: 1 Maccabees deals with the period from the outbreak of the rebellion down to the death of Simon and accession of John Hyrcanus; the other devotes much more attention to the events, especially the persecutions, which led up to the outbreak, and then deals only with the

the king's officials arrived at their village of Modein, they put them to death, and then took to the hills and gathered round them all who felt that their only hope lay in armed rebellion.

Judas, one of the five brothers, put himself at the head of this small group of men. A few quick victories against local Greek forces, and ruthless action against those Jews who had collaborated with the enemy, spread the reputation of the band, and volunteers flowed in to swell their numbers. Even so, the Jewish forces were no match for the Seleucid armies. Judas was undoubtedly a man of great courage and skill, and used his familiarity with the difficult terrain in the hills to engage in guerilla warfare in which the enemy's superiority of forces was of less advantage. Nevertheless, he could hardly have had much success if the Seleucids had not at that time been occupied in warfare against the Parthians. Even so, Antiochus was able to send a force of several thousands to deal with the rebellion. Judas' defeat of this army was his first great victory; and when in the following year he defeated an even greater force, the way was open for him to march on Jerusalem. He was not able to take the Acra, but he was able to cleanse

------

campaigns of Judas, ending with his liberation of Jerusalem.

the Temple of its pagan defilements, and rededicate it to the service of God. This date, December, 164, was thereafter commemorated in the Feast of the Dedication.

Judas then pressed forward his success. To Galilee, across the Jordan, to Philistia his forces went to liberate the faithful Jews from the oppression of the Hellenists. Then he turned his attention to the Acra. But the Seleucids were not willing to see this foothold in Jerusalem go. Antiochus IV had died in the Parthian war and had been succeeded by an eight-year-old son, but the general, Lysias, was acting as regent and he now made a determined attempt to crush the revolt. He drove the Jewish forces back in an attack from the south, and forced them to retreat until they took refuge in Jerusalem. Lysias then prepared for a final assault. But once more the Jews were saved by the internal difficulties of the Seleucids in the form of a rival claimant to the power of Lysias. The regent therefore offered acceptable terms to the besieged Jews, including the abrogation of the decrees of Antiochus IV which had sparked off the rebellion, and withdrew his forces.

It is probably from this moment that we can date a change of policy in the conduct of the Maccabees, a change which was to lead to sad consequences. The rebellion had now achieved all that could be hoped for—a measure of political liberty and above all religious independence. It was reasonable therefore to cease the conflict. Certainly there were many Jews who expected this. But Judas had now set his sights on a wider goal, nothing less than complete political independence, the restoration of Israel to something like its former glory.

He therefore decided to continue the struggle. In the first battles he repeated his former successes; but finally in 160, the Greeks assembled a force which Judas's followers had no stomach to face; Judas and a small band of faithful adherents nevertheless plunged bravely into battle, and Judas himself was killed.

Once again the Greeks were willing to settle affairs on terms which would meet all reasonable Jewish hopes; but once more a small band of fanatics, with Judas's brother Jonathan at their head, preferred to carry on the struggle. For some years they could do little more than harass an enemy who was not strongly entrenched in the land. But yet again the turn of events came to their aid, and this time decisively. There were at this time two claimants to the Seleucid throne, and both of them realized that Jonathan's small band could be a useful pawn in their game. With astonishing boldness Jonathan played both sides off against each other as they raised their bid in an attempt to ensure his support. At the end of this bargaining, Jonathan found himself in a stronger position than that which had been won by the previous years of hard fighting: he was given permission to maintain an army, the Seleucids agreed to remove most of their garrisons, while Jonathan was given control of Jerusalem, recognized as ruler of the new Jewish state and "appointed" high priest. To be fair to Jonathan —whose conduct savours unpleasantly of duplicity and opportunism—he did loyally support the side he eventually opted for; and in the warfare which followed he was rewarded with further extension of his territories.

The position of the Jews—and of the Maccabees at their head—was now assured. When Jonathan himself died (a victim, ironically, of the rivalry and treachery in Greek domestic politics which had previously served him so well), his brother Simon succeeded without too much difficulty. Simon ruled—and it is significant that we can now speak of ruling, not merely of leading a rebellion—for some ten years, for the most part successfully. He was assassinated in 134 by his own son-in-law; and his son John Hyrcanus I succeeded to his titles and positions as accepted dynastic heir.

The Hasmoneans, as the new dynasty was called, proceeded on a course whose direction

could already have been foreseen. Their title of
high priest, head of a religious community, became increasingly a religious fiction; in fact they
were secular monarchs with the trappings, ambitions and eventually even the title of "king".
They continued the aggressive, warlike policy of
the Maccabees, but not now with any pretence
that this was necessary for the defence of their
faith or even their country, but simply for the
extension of their power. These wars were
fought with mercenary troops, not with a
popular army. One such conquest was to be
particularly significant in subsequent history;
this was the conquest of Idumea, ancient Edom,
which John Hyrcanus annexed, forcing the
people to a nominal acceptance of the Jewish
faith.

Hyrcanus was succeeded by his son Aristobulos, who reigned for a year and was followed
by his brother Alexander Jannaeus. His reign
makes it evident how far the new regime had
gone and how great was the gulf between ruler
and people. Alexander continued the aggressive
wars of his predecessors; but he was so clearly a
typical oriental king that the Jews deeply re-
sented the scandal caused when occasionally he
appeared in his role of high priest. They even
appealed to the Seleucid king of the time to
come to their aid and depose this tyrant.

Alexander on his side responded with contempt, and maintained control by force and terror, so that he came to be regarded as an oppressor equal to the hated Antiochus Epiphanes: a startling reversal of roles for a grandson of the Maccabees in less than a century from that glorious war of liberation.

After the death of Alexander Jannaeus in 76, his wife Alexandra Salome took over the government of the country, reserving the position of high priest for her son, Hyrcanus II. Her prudent and conciliatory measures did something to allay the dangerous discontent which her husband had left behind him. But after her death, events moved quickly to a strange conclusion. Her son, Hyrcanus II, was the natural successor; but he was a lethargic character and was challenged for possession by his younger brother Aristobulos II. But Antipater, the ambitious and astute governor of the recently annexed Idumea, saw in this situation an opportunity to exercise his peculiar talents and to turn the tables on his masters. He stirred Hyrcanus to resist the claims of his brother, and thus sparked off a civil war which threatened the peace of the area and thus attracted the attention of the Romans.

Rome had for some time played a part in affairs in Asia—we have seen that she was indirectly concerned in the events which led to the

Maccabean outbreak—but as the empire extended further eastwards, she began to play an even more active part. The Roman armies under Pompey conquered Pontus and Armenia, and this led to a general reorganization of their eastern possessions. The remnant of the Seleucid Empire was replaced by the Roman Province of Syria; and it was this which justified interference in the troubled affairs of Judah. The solution imposed by Pompey—largely through the influence of Antipater—was to confirm the position of Hyrcanus. This decision was not accepted peacefully, and Pompey had to follow it up with a show of force, in the course of which he shocked Jewish susceptibilities by entering the Holy of Holies in the Temple.

But these were troubled times for Rome too, with Pompey and Caesar, Lepidus, Cassius, Antony and Octavius involved in a complicated pattern of rivalry and alliance. In this confusion there were rich rewards for anyone with the courage, acumen and good fortune to be on the winning side. This was a game which suited admirably the cunning of the Idumeans. Hyrcanus retained the nominal position of high priest, but it became more and more clear that the real power lay with Antipater. His support of Caesar against Pompey was rewarded with the post of Procurator of Judaea, and in this role he appointed his young son Herod to administer Galilee for him. After Antipater's death, Herod showed the same skill in intrigue, the same adroitness in seeing through the maze of Roman politics and emerging as supporter of the successful party. The result must have surpassed even his expectations. In 40 BC, Herod was appointed King of the Jews.

There we may leave the study of the political events of Jewish history—not merely because during Herod's reign the history of the People of God enters a new phase, which we call the New Testament; but also because, as we shall now see, the political events have become more and more irrelevant to the real life of Israel.

### 3. SHEEP WITHOUT A SHEPHERD

The attitude of the post-exilic community was inward-looking, withdrawn as far as possible from the world outside. The whole of life— public and private, political and religious—was to be regulated by the Law of God. As befitted such a religious community, the priests, with the high priest at their head, were the authorities; but since in practice the Law was supreme, the experts in the Law had a great deal of influence, and these experts were not necessarily priests but could come from any class of the people.

These men were the embodiment of the conservative element in Judaism, the guardians of tradition and masters of its interpretation. Their zeal concerned itself above all with the rules which the Law laid down. They made it their task to erect a "hedge" round the Laws, as one of their number put it, a hedge of secondary precepts, deductions and casuistry which would protect it from infringement. Infringement of the Law involved legal "uncleanness", and in a pagan environment especially it was practically impossible, without this expertise and hairsplitting, to avoid defilement. The ordinary people did in fact incur defilement— they were "the accursed mob which knows not the Law". (John 7.49.) It was probably for this reason that this party became known as the "Pharisees", those who are apart, cut off from the defilement of the world.

In this concept of "uncleanness", the main factor was not moral fault but separation from the full life of the community which could only be regained by a certain number of ritual actions, washings particularly. This idea—to some extent a derivation from the ancient idea of "holiness" —had a valuable part to play in Israel's moral education. (See p. 119.) But in applying it mechanically without regard for changed circumstances and above all without regard for the spirit of the Law, the Pharisees were in danger of reducing religion to a matter of external forms —a fault against which the Prophets had inveighed—with the Law now playing the part which sacrifice played then. This could lead to a still more serious distortion of Israel's religion, which again the Prophets had foreseen. Religion is a personal relationship based on love —"mercy and not sacrifice", as Hosea put it. But the Pharisaic attitude would treat religion as an impersonal contractual relationship, a bargain, in which man's service demanded divine repayment. It was the realization of this error that struck the convert Pharisee Paul of Tarsus so deeply that he made it the basis for his polemic against his former colleagues. (Cf. Rom. 4.1–16.) At its best, this could lead to complacency and pride. At its worst, it could lead to hypocrisy: the Laws, interpreted as the Pharisees interpreted it, was so great a burden that it was almost physically impossible to observe it completely, and the temptation remained to preserve the outward show of observance empty not only of the spirit but even of the letter, leaving a spiritual state which could aptly be described as that of "whited sepulchres".

Such an attitude, though always a danger in Judaism (as it is for any religious system), was not endemic in Israel, and there were always some who ridiculed its exaggerations. A more liberal mentality, moreover, was fostered by the inescapable influence of Hellenism. The priests in particular were of this cast of mind—partly, no doubt, simply through opposition to the predominantly lay Pharisee movement which had usurped much of their authority, and partly because their position brought them, more than most, into contact with the pagan authorities and the non-Jewish world and led them to see the need for some sort of accommodation to this world. It was probably for this reason, because of the number of priests who shared such views, that this party was known as the "Sadducees", from the name of David's priest Zadok, from whom the post-exilic priests claimed descent. They had none of the legal fanaticism of the Pharisees; they minimised rather than extended the scope of the Law—the official Scriptures, of course, had to be accepted, but not the oral traditions treasured by the Pharisees nor late developments in doctrine, such as belief in the resurrection or in angels.

The opposition between these two groups, the Pharisees and Sadducees, must not be stressed too much. There was certainly no question of religious schism in which one side was the bulwark of orthodoxy and the other was propagating heresy. It was not even a question of two parties so much as of schools of thought or attitudes of mind. Both Pharisees and Sadducees, for example, were represented on the Sanhedrin, the council which assisted the high priest in policy-making and legislation for Judah's internal affairs.

Moreover, even among the traditionalists, not all were of the same mind. Even at the time of persecution by Antiochus Epiphanes, loyalty to the ancestral faith expressed itself in different ways; besides the Maccabees, who chose to resist by force of arms, there were the Hasidim, who preferred death or flight. The Pharisees were in a sense the heirs of the Maccabean spirit; they too gave expression to their faith by action, though this action was now political rather than military. For the law of God, they held, was still the only law of the Jewish state, and in accordance with this conviction they held themselves justified and even bound to control or influence the political affairs of the nation. It was they who led the opposition to the Hasmoneans, incurring the hatred and persecution of Alexander Jannaeus; and it was by conciliating them that Alexandra Salome was able to rule without too much opposition. But the Hasidim had their spiritual heirs too, those who felt that the Pharisees were not separatist enough, that the holiness of the true Israel demanded an even greater abstention from the affairs of the world. This feeling became stronger when experience of the Hasmonean tyranny showed what could happen when resistance to the outside world took the form of military or political activity. The only solution, some felt, was complete withdrawal from the world. One such group retired to the wilderness of Judah, and settled at Khirbet Qumran on the shores of the Dead Sea. There they carried on an almost monastic existence, in which celibacy and community of property were held in high regard. This sect is another warning against oversimplifying the divisions of party and opinion which existed at that time. Like the Sadducees, this sect, too, included many priests; a great interest in matters of sacrifice and liturgy is characteristic of their teachings, and at least at one period of their history they seem to have called themselves by the same sort of name, the "Zadokites". But in their general spirit and in some of their practices they were even more akin to the Pharisees. They looked on themselves as the only true Israelites, the community of the new covenant; they held that in themselves the ancient prophecies were fulfilled, and interpreted the Scriptures in this spirit; and from their midst, as they prepared in the desert the way of the Lord, they looked for two leaders to arise, one of priestly rank, the other representing the secular arm, a Messiah of Aaron and a Messiah of David, to usher in God's kingdom.

In this at least all schools of thought found common ground, that they all had their gaze fixed on the future. Israel was a religion of hope. From the very fact and nature of their origin, they had a sense of destiny; God's first intervention at the Exodus was the pledge of further intervention; it was the source of an awareness of history, of time which had a beginning and would have an end. This end, "the last days", would certainly involve some definitive intervention of God, the establishment of his kingdom. What exactly this would involve was a matter of speculation and dispute. For some, it would be something primarily spiritual: God's Spirit, which had moved over the waters at creation, which had filled the Judges with God's power, which had spoken through the Prophets, would now be poured out on all men (Joel 3.2), cleansing men's hearts and giving them a new life. (Cf. Ezek. 36.26.) For others, the majority, the coming of the Kingdom of God would include at least some political element, in which the pagans would either be converted to the true faith or made subject to a triumphant Israel. Usually, too, it was thought that God would use some human intermediary in fulfilling his plan, someone like the great figures of

old; a new David, a Messiah; or a prophet like
Moses; or even a "Son of Man", according to a
train of thought which developed the idea of
Daniel 7.13. The apocalyptic literature of this
time attempted to describe in dramatic imagery
the character and even the time of this final
intervention of God; and the popularity of this
type of literature at the end of the Old-Testament period, wild and fantastic though much of
it was, at least testifies to the fervent desire that
God should complete his work, at that time so
evidently and so sadly incomplete.[4]

But underneath these more or less definable
parties we have been discussing, there was the
vast anonymous mass of the people, especially
those of the *diaspora*, which now outnumbered
those in Palestine itself. Even in the *diaspora*
these schools of thought were not unknown; Saul
of Tarsus, for example, boasted that he was a
Pharisee. But for the vast majority of the people,
these party rivalries were a matter of little concern; while aristocratic Sadducees and fanatical
Pharisees both, though for different reasons, regarded them with contempt. Deserted and
ignored by those who should have been their
leaders, the people had to live their lives and
nourish their faith as best they could; and for

[4] Cf. H. H. Rowley, *The Relevance of Apocalyptic*,
(1944).

this they turned to the real source of Israel's life, the word of God. The great feasts united them with God's great deeds of the past; the Prophets spoke to them again; and through the Psalms they prayed with the authentic voice of Israel. In them, the soul of Israel lived on. But it was a soul without a body.

A soul without a body, or a body without a head. At the term of Israel's history, we have the impression of a community that is strangely lost, groping and uncertain of its way. In the first period of their history, after the Exodus, one could say with confidence that this was an amphictyony, a people bound together in covenant; later, it was equally clear that they were a monarchy; even after the Exile, the community had some recognizable form which corresponded to its life at that time—a religious community, what is often called a theocracy. But now the political institutions in which they lived bore little relationship to their true life. The Hasmoneans, and still more Herod, made no pretence to be the successors of David and the people tolerated their rule without feeling that it in any way involved the destiny of Israel. The Romans were simply foreign invaders, an alien occupying force; and the day when people could cry, "We have no king but Caesar", would be the day when they denied their own destiny. For the worldly but powerful Sadducees, they could have only contempt and suspicion. For the arrogant Pharisees, they might have respect and sometimes admiration; they would recognize that they sat in the chair of Moses, but in their petty casuistry they could not hear a voice which spoke as one having authority.

A body without a head, sheep without a shepherd. But the Lord is their shepherd; from the day when he first led them out into the desert, he has not ceased to guide and feed them. Their history is nothing else than the story of God's abiding presence with them. It is the repeated assurance that he is faithful and true; that he will be mindful of their fathers; that he will visit and redeem his people.

# ARCHAEOLOGICAL PERIODS

| | |
|---|---|
| Paleolithic | ending about 10,000 BC |
| Mesolithic | about 10,000–8000 BC (early villages) |
| Neolithic | about 8000–5000 BC (pottery) |
| Chalcolithic | about 5000–3500 BC |
| Early Bronze | 3500–2200 BC |
| Middle Bronze | 2100–1500 BC (nomadic incursions; period of Israel's ancestors) |
| Late Bronze | 1500–1200 BC |
| Iron Age | 1200–330 BC |
| Hellenistic Era | 330 to the Roman and Christian period |

# CHRONOLOGICAL TABLE

| | 2000 | |
|---|---|---|
| The Egyptian Middle Kingdom exercised some control of Palestine: but increasing Amorite pressure in Palestine and Mesopotamia | | |
| 1720–1560: Hyksos in Egypt. Hammurabi founds the first Babylonian Empire, about 1700 | 1700 | The Patriarchs in Canaan<br><br>Jacob's descendants in Egypt |
| Hyksos driven out of Egypt about 1560; Egyptian campaigns in Palestine and Syria | | |
| Kingdom of Mitanni formed about this time | 1500 | |
| Amarna period<br>Akhenaten, 1377–1358 | 1400 | |
| Ramesses II, 1302–1234<br>Treaty between Egypt and Hittites | 1300 | The Exodus, Covenant at Sinai |
| Peoples of the Sea attack Egypt | 1200 | Invasion of Canaan |
| | | Philistines in Canaan<br>Period of Judges |
| Arameans in Mesopotamia | 1100 | |
| | 1000 | Saul, 1030–1010<br>David, 1010–970<br>Solomon, 970–931 |
| | 900 | 931–721: Divided Kingdom, see p. 140 |
| Shishak of Egypt invades Palestine | | Omri, 876–869 |
| Ashurnasirpal, 883–859<br>Shalmaneser III, 858–824 | | |
| | 800 | |
| Battle of Qarqar, 853 | | Isaiah |

| | | |
|---|---|---|
| Tiglath Pileser III, 745–727 | 700 | Fall of Samaria, 721 |
| Sargon II, 721–705 | | Hezekiah King of Judah, 716–687 |
| Ashurbanipal, 668–621 | | 621, Josiah's reform |
| 609: beginning of Babylonian Empire | | 609, Battle of Megiddo, death of Josiah |
| | 600 | |
| Nebuchadnezzar, 604–562 | | 587, destruction of Jerusalem |
| Nabonidus, 555–539 | | 587–538, exile |
| Cyrus, 539–529 | | Second Isaiah |
| Darius I, 522–486 | | 538, first exiles return |
| Marathon, 490 | | Haggai, Zechariah |
| Salamis, 480 | 500 | 515, completion of Temple |
| Artaxerxes I, 465–423 | | 445, Nehemiah |
| Artaxerxes II, 404–358 | 400 | 428, Ezra (?) |
| Plato, 429–347 | | |
| 323, death of Alexander the Great | 300 | |
| Antiochus III, 223–187 | 200 | |
| 188, Antiochus defeated by Romans | | 197, Judea under the Seleucids |
| Antiochus IV Epiphanes, 175–164 | | Persecution of the Jews |
| | | 166, Rebellion of Maccabees |
| | 160 | 160, death of Judas |
| | 150 | |
| | | 143, death of Jonathan |
| | 140 | |
| | 130 | John Hyrcanus I, 134–104 |
| | 120 | |
| | 110 | |
| | | Alexander Jannaeus, 104–76 |
| | 100 | |
| 66–62, Pompey's campaigns | | |
| 48, Caesar's victory at Pharsalus | | |
| | | Herod the Great, 40–4 |

The information on these maps has been intentionally kept to the minimum, since their purpose is simply to give the reader a clear indication of the geographical background to the history, and especially to the relationship between Israel and her neighbours. There are many good biblical atlases available today to which the reader may refer for more detailed information—for example *The Westminster Historical Atlas of the Bible*, ed. G. E. Wright and F. V. Filson, London, S.C.M. Press; L. H. Grollenberg, *Atlas of the Bible*, trans. and ed. H. H. Rowley and Joyce M. H. Reid, London and Edinburgh, Nelson; *Oxford Bible Atlas*, ed. H. G. May, R. W. Hamilton and G. N. S. Hunt, O.U.P.

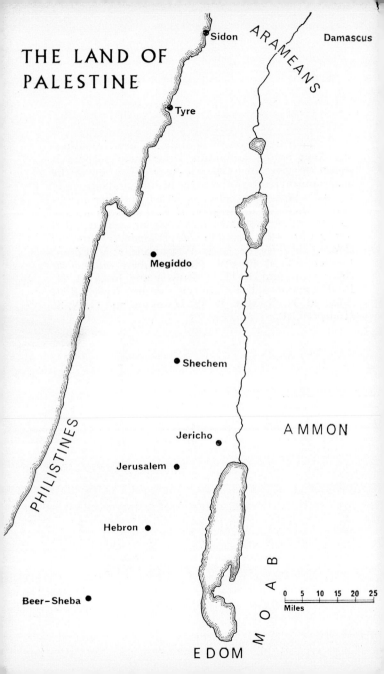

# THE LAND OF PALESTINE

Sidon

ARAMEANS

Damascus

Tyre

Megiddo

Shechem

PHILISTINES

Jericho

AMMON

Jerusalem

Hebron

Beer-Sheba

EDOM

MOAB

0   5   10   15   20   25
Miles

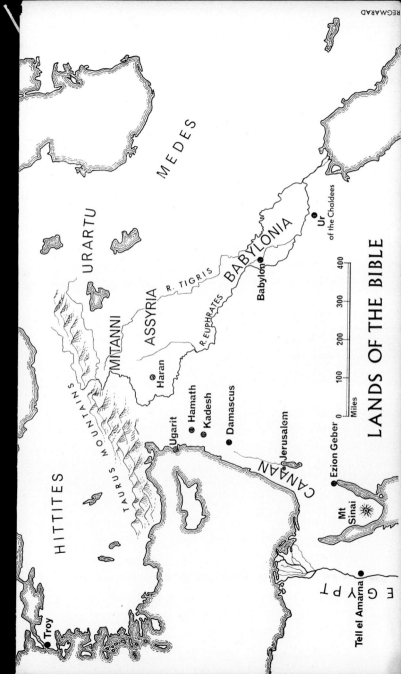

LANDS OF THE BIBLE

Troy

HITTITES

URARTU

MEDES

TAURUS MOUNTAINS

MITANNI

ASSYRIA

R. TIGRIS

R. EUPHRATES

BABYLONIA

Babylon

Ur
of the Chaldees

Haran

Ugarit

Hamath
Kadesh
Damascus

Jerusalem

CANAAN

Ezion Geber

Mt
Sinai

EGYPT

Tell el Amarna

0    100   200   300   400
Miles

REGMARAD